Coward

Coward

Coward

Coward

Coward

Coward

Coward

Colors by Val Staples

Coward

A **CRIMINAL** edition by Ed Brubaker and Sean Phillips

Introduction

Survival.

That's what it's all about, right?

Leo is a man who knows instinctively when and how to walk/run/get away. For this talent, he is branded a coward.

But a coward only cares about himself. Leo struggles to help people -- or, at least, the walking wounded who dwell in the same shadows, who face the same dangers as he does.

Why?

Because his survival is based, not solely on his own instincts, but on the sacrifices of others.

His failures cut as deeply into his skin as a shard of glass or a bullet. His failures force him to break his own carefully-designed set of rules; rules which guarantee that he will see another sunrise.

If life is only about survival, then what is the ultimate cost?

Does what it take to survive change you -- to the point where you are no longer who you are? To the point where, though your body survives, the deepest part of you -- the human part -- does not?

A body is a temporary thing. We like to think a soul lasts forever. And so, our actions matter.

A true coward can't face the reality of that.

Tom Fontana

Tom Fontana is the multiple Emmy, Peabody, and Writer's Guild Award-Winning writer and creator of the ground-breaking TV series Homicide: Life on the Streets and OZ.

Prologue

WHENEVER THINGS BEGIN TO FALL TO PIECES, I THINK OF MY FATHER

NOT HIM AND IVAN IN THE EARLY DAYS, WORKING THE CROWDS.

NO, I THINK OF THE BIG JOBS, WHEN I'D HEAR HIM AND HIS FRIENDS ARGUING IN THE BASEMENT...

HEARING PLANS GOING OFF THE RAILS, HEARING GLASS BREAKING...

HEARING DEATH IN THE VOICES OF THE MEN HE WAS WORKING WITH.

THEN ME AND RICKY LAWLESS, WE'D ESCAPE INTO THE NIGHT...

INTO THE BACKSTREETS.

JUNKYARD DOGS AT OUR HEELS.

THE NIGHT AIR FULL OF POSSIBILITY AND FEAR

BUT WE DIDN'T CARE.

WE WERE KIDS, WE HAD NO RULES.

NOT SOCIETY'S, FOR DAMN SURE.

RULES CAME LATER

AFTER MY FATHER WENT AWAY FOR BREAKING HIS OWN.

THAT'S WHEN IVAN EXPLAINED IT TO ME, ABOUT THE RULES AND HOW THEY PROTECT YOU...

SOMETIMES EVEN FROM YOURSELF.

YOU LEARN THESE RULES OVER TIME, THROUGH HARD EXPERIENCE.

AND YOU NEVER WRITE THEM DOWN, BUT YOU NEVER FORGET THEM.

THEY'RE THE RULES THAT WILL KEEP YOU OUT IN THE WORLD.

SAFE.

THEY'RE WHAT SEPARATES A PROFESSIONAL FROM A PUNK/PIMP/GANGSTA/LOWRIDER WITH A GUN.

THOSE IDIOTS ARE CANNON-FODDER FOR THE SYSTEM.

BUT SOMEONE WHO FOLLOWS THE RULES, WHO UNDERSTANDS HOW TO STAY SAFE...

... WILL NEVER ROT TO DEATH IN A 4 X 5 CEMENT ROOM.

SOMETIMES I TELL PEOPLE ABOUT THE RULES AND THEY ASK WHAT I'M SO SCARED OF...

AND I TELL THEM.

I'M SCARED OF ENDING UP LIKE MY FATHER.

SCARED OF DYING WHERE I MOST LIKELY BELONG... IN PRISON.

BUT THE WAY I SEE IT... IF YOU AREN'T SCARED, IN OUR LINE OF WORK, THEN YOU JUST AREN'T THINKING.

AND I WON'T WORK WITH PEOPLE WHO DON'T USE THEIR BRAINS BEFORE THEIR BULLETS...

...AS A RULE, AT LEAST.

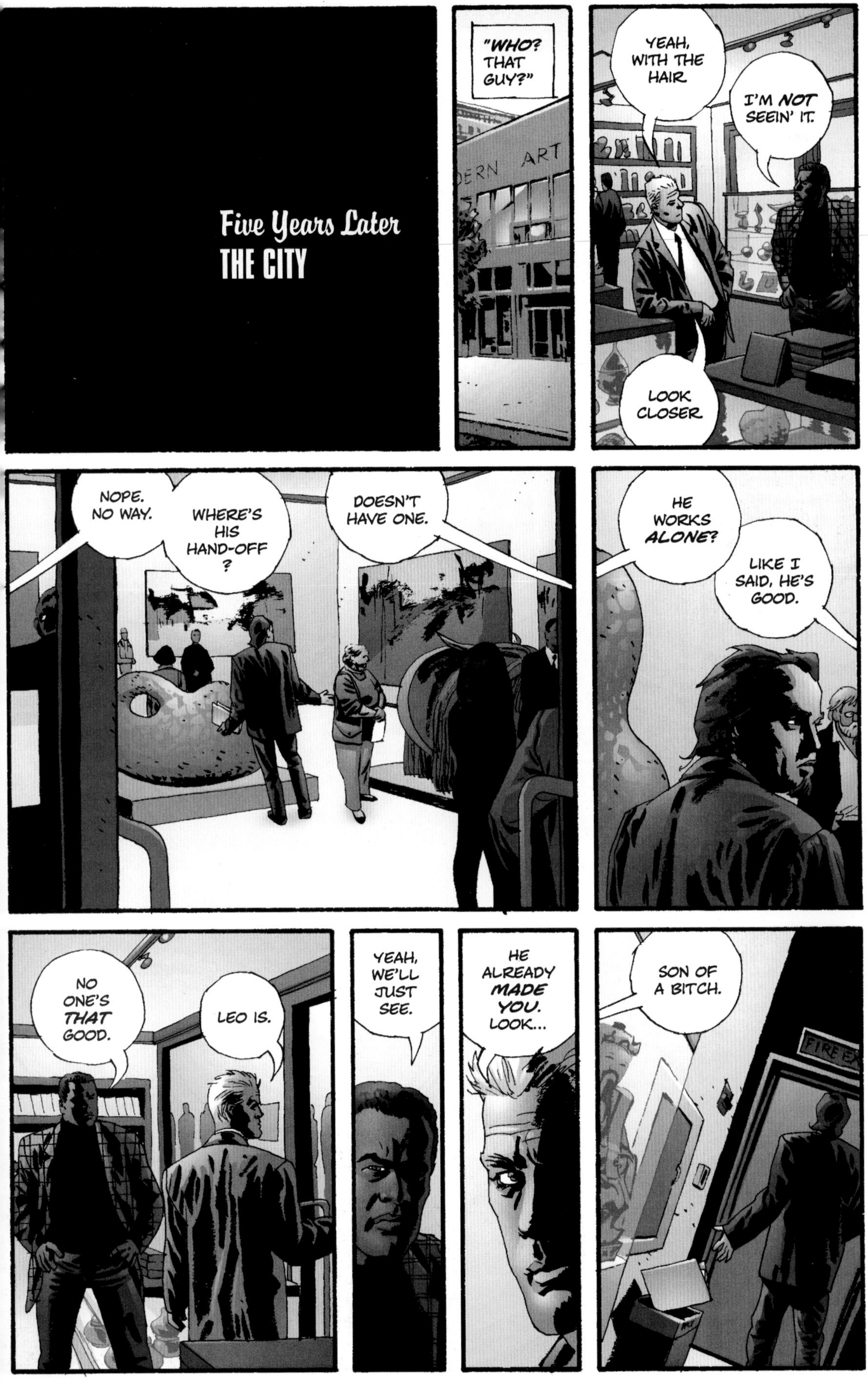
Five Years Later
THE CITY
"WHO? THAT GUY?"
YEAH, WITH THE HAIR
I'M NOT SEEIN' IT.
LOOK CLOSER
NOPE. NO WAY.
WHERE'S HIS HAND-OFF?
DOESN'T HAVE ONE.
HE WORKS ALONE?
LIKE I SAID, HE'S GOOD.
NO ONE'S THAT GOOD.
LEO IS.
YEAH, WE'LL JUST SEE.
HE ALREADY MADE YOU. LOOK...
SON OF A BITCH.

HEY -- HEY *YOU*, HOLD IT.

YEAH?

POLICE. GRAB THE WALL, ASSHOLE.

DID I *DO* SOMETHING?

GRAB THE FUCKING WALL.

THIS MUST BE A *MISTAKE*, OFFICER... I DON'T -

YOU LIKE THOSE *TEETH*? THEN SHUT 'EM.

YOU'RE WASTING YOUR *TIME*, JEFF...

...HE DUMPED IT ALL INSIDE. I *TOLD YOU* HE WAS GOOD.

HELLO, LEO.

FUCKING *SEYMOUR*.

THIS GUY EVEN A *REAL COP*?

YEAH, HE IS.

LET'S TAKE A WALK.

WHAT THE HELL **IS THIS**, LEO? THESE WALLETS ARE PRACTICALLY EMPTY.

BUT YOU KNOW RICH PEOPLE DON'T CARRY **CASH**, THAT'S HOW THEY STAY RICH.

SO WHAT'RE YOU **UP TO**?

LIKE I'M GONNA TELL YOU AND **CAPTAIN BADGE** HERE.

HE'S MORE LIKE CAPTAIN **BEATDOWN**, ACTUALLY.

AND UNLESS YOU WANT ME TO CAVE IN YOUR SKULL, ANSWER THE FUCKING QUESTION.

IT'S NOT ABOUT HOW MUCH CASH THEY'RE CARRYING, SEYMOUR.

IT'S ABOUT **IDENTITY THEFT**.

TOURISTS NEVER HAVE MORE THAN A FEW HUNDRED, BUT **THOSE** PEOPLE...

I CAN GET A THOUSAND A POP FOR THEIR CARDS AND ID.

SEE, JEFF? HE'S ALWAYS **THINKIN'**.

WHAT DO YOU **WANT**, SEYMOUR?

I'M PUTTING TOGETHER A TEAM.

I'M *OUT* OF THAT LINE OF WORK.

'CAUSE OF THE SALT BAY JOB?

WHAT DO *YOU* THINK?

I THINK YOU AN' ME WERE THE ONLY SMART PEOPLE *THERE* THAT DAY.

WHICH IS WHY WE *NEED* YOU.

EVEN *IF* I WAS STILL WORKING... YOU *KNOW* I DON'T WORK WITH *COPS.*

NO MATTER HOW BENT THEY ARE.

JUST HEAR ME OUT. THIS IS *BIG TIME.*

AND IT'S EASY PICKING...

...OR, IT WILL BE FOR *YOU.*

I'M *LISTENING...* BUT THE ANSWER WON'T CHANGE.

NOT EVEN FOR FIVE MILLION IN DIAMONDS?

YEAH? AND WHAT DIAMONDS ARE *EVER* EASY PICKING?

ONES IN A *POLICE EVIDENCE VAN* ON THE WAY TO COURT.

THAT'S WHY JEFF IS HERE. IT'S *HIS* SCORE.

BUT I NEED *YOU*. I NEED YOUR *EYES*.

YOU MUST'VE LOST YOUR *MIND* IN THE LAST FIVE YEARS, SEYMOUR

I'LL LOOK FOR YOUR *SUICIDE BY COP* IN THE PAPERS.

NOW CAN I HAVE MY SHIT BACK?

FUCK OFF.

FINE, WHATEVER

LOOK, JUST *THINK* ABOUT IT. GIVE IT A DAY.

THIS IS *REAL*... AND *INSIDE HELP* FROM A GUY LIKE JEFF IS THE *ONLY WAY* TO WORK IT.

I'LL SEEYA, SEYMOUR

THE FUCK WAS *THAT*? SHOULDA LET ME HIT HIM.

NAH. HE'LL COME AROUND, DON'T WORRY.

I GOT A BACK-UP PLAN...

SEYMOUR *WAS* A SMART GUY, BUT HE WAS A GAMBLER, TOO. HE PLAYED THE ODDS ON HIS SCORES, FIGURING THE TAKE WAS USUALLY WORTH THE RISK.

THAT'S WHY I STEERED CLEAR OF HIM. GAMBLERS GOT YOU RICH *OR* THEY GOT YOU *KILLED.*

THE LAST JOB I WORKED WITH SEYMOUR, PEOPLE DIED.

NOT REALLY HIS FAULT, BUT STILL... IT WAS *HIS* SCORE.

AND HIS FACE WAS THE LAST THING I NEEDED TO SEE.

HIS GODDAMN GHOULISH GRIN... HIS SMUG COP BUDDY.

I GUESS HE *FORGOT* WHAT THE COPS IN THIS CITY HAD *DONE* TO MOST OF OUR FRIENDS.

BUT I'D **NEVER** FORGET.

I COULD STILL SEE THEM... ON THE EMPTY BARSTOOLS AT THE **UNDERTOW**... IN THE FACES OF THEIR WIDOWS AND CHILDREN...

THEY'D BEEN YANKED OUT OF THIS WORLD SO EASILY...

...AND THE HOLES THEY LEFT BEHIND... IN LIFE, IN MEMORY, IN DREAMS...

...THOSE WOUNDS WERE SCARS THAT'D BE EASIER TO HIDE, BUT THEY WERE SCARS ALL THE SAME.

NO, I DIDN'T NEED TO SEE SEYMOUR'S FACE... AND I DIDN'T NEED HIS 'EASY' SCORE.

I HAD ENOUGH TROUBLE OF MY OWN TO DEAL WITH.

NO! NOT ONE MORE DAY!

DO YOU KNOW WHAT THE LITTLE PERV *DID* TO ME?

JUST —

HE TOOK MY *UNDERWEAR!* JUST MADE 'EM DISAPPEAR!

IVAN.

WHAT? THEY'RE RIGHT HERE...

LISTEN, I'M REALLY SORRY ABOUT THIS...

I KNOW HE'S A LOT TO HANDLE SOMETIMES...

SOMETIMES? HE SHOULD BE IN A *STRAIGHTJACKET.*

THAT PROBABLY WOULDN'T DO MUCH GOOD.

I DON'T EVEN WANT TO *TELL YOU* HOW I REALIZED HE'D *PANTSED* ME.

JUST... I KNOW... *OKAY?* BUT HE'S A SICK OLD MAN.

JUST STAY ANOTHER *WEEK,* UNTIL I CAN FIND SOMEONE ELSE...

I'M SORRY, LEO... HE'S JUST TOO MUCH.

HE SHOULD BE IN A *HOME*... ONE WITH ALL *MALE* NURSES.

I CAN'T AFFORD THAT... NOT THE KIND OF PLACE HE'D NEED.

WITH HIS... *QUIRKS*.

THEN YOU NEED TO GET HIM CLEAN, LEO.

BUT WHATEVER YOU DO, YOU'LL HAVE TO FIND SOMEONE *ELSE* FOR TOMORROW.

'CAUSE IF HE TOUCHED ME AGAIN, I'M AFRAID I'LL KILL HIM.

NICE, IVAN... REAL NICE.

WHAT DID I *DO*, TOMMY?

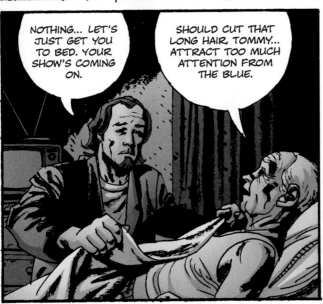

NOTHING... LET'S JUST GET YOU TO BED. YOUR SHOW'S COMING ON.

SHOULD CUT THAT LONG HAIR, TOMMY... ATTRACT TOO MUCH ATTENTION FROM THE BLUE.

I WILL... TOMORROW.

I PROMISE.

TOMMY WAS MY DAD.

BUT HE'D BEEN DEAD A LONG TIME.

BACK BEFORE IVAN GOT LOST IN HIS JUNK HABIT...

BEFORE *ALZHEIMER'S* CAME AND TOOK HIM EVEN FURTHER AWAY.

I WOULDN'T KNOW HOW TO GET HIM CLEAN NOW, EVEN IF I WANTED TO.

IT'D BE *TORTURE*, AND HE'D HAVE NO IDEA WHY IT WAS HAPPENING.

BUT HE BURNS THROUGH PRIVATE NURSES LIKE NOBODY'S BUSINESS.

HE THINKS HE'S THIRTY YEARS OLD, SO HE'S CONSTANTLY TRYING TO BANG THEM.

IT'S ALMOST FUNNY, BUT IT'S NOT.

KNKK
KNKK

UH... YEAH?

DO YOU REMEMBER ME, ASSHOLE?

41

REMEMBER *TERRY WATSON?*

TERRY WATSON.

WHAT DO YOU **WANT**, GRETA?

I WANT TO BE ABLE TO GET MY **DAUGHTER** OUT OF THIS CITY, LEO.

SO SHE CAN HAVE A REAL LIFE.

DID I MISS THE **FIRST PART** OF THIS CONVERSATION?

SEYMOUR'S **JOB**.

HE SAYS HE **NEEDS YOU** TO MAKE IT WORK AND YOU'RE BEING A **PUNK**.

LET'S TAKE A WALK.

IT'S RAINING.

IT'LL BE A **SHORT** WALK.

WOULD YOU **SLOW DOWN**? A LITTLE?

HOW'D YOU FIND MY **ROOM**?

DOES **SEYMOUR** KNOW WHERE I LIVE?

GROW A BRAIN. IF SEYMOUR KNEW WHERE TO FIND YOU ON *HIS OWN*, HE WOULDN'T *NEED* ME...

...WOULD HE?

THAT'S HOW THEY KNEW I'D BE AT THE *MODERN?*

YOU'VE BEEN FOLLOWING ME?

I'M ONLY *IN* ON THIS JOB BECAUSE I PROMISED I COULD FIND *YOU.*

TOOK SOME EFFORT, THOUGH, I'LL GIVE YOU THAT.

DAMN IT... I ALREADY TOLD SEYMOUR -- HE JUST...

HE TAKES TOO MANY CHANCES.

BULLSHIT! YOU'RE THE ONE WHO *SHUT ME OUT!*

IF I'D BEEN IN *SALT BAY* THAT DAY, I WOULDN'T BE A *SINGLE MOTHER!*

I TOLD YOU THEN, I DON'T WORK WITH *JUNKIES.* IT'S A RULE.

FUCK YOUR *RULES!* I'VE BEEN SOBER FOR FUCKING *YEARS!*

I HAD A *BABY,* ASSHOLE! I HAD *KICKED!*

NO ONE EVER *REALLY* KICKS...

THEY'RE RIGHT, WHAT THEY *SAY* ABOUT YOU, AREN'T THEY?

TERRY ALWAYS SAID IT WAS *BULLSHIT,* BUT THEY'RE *RIGHT.*

AND HE PAID FOR THAT...

TWO HOURS LATER, AGAINST MY BETTER JUDGMENT, I'M WALKING INTO *THE UNDERTOW.*

THE JUKEBOX HASN'T CHANGED SINCE THE LAST TIME I WAS HERE.

HELL, IT HASN'T CHANGED SINCE THE *FIRST TIME* I WAS HERE, AND I WAS EIGHT YEARS OLD THEN.

IT'S THE SAME SMOKY CROONERS AND DEPRESSIVES THAT MAKE A DARK BARROOM EVEN DARKER

GNARLY'S ON DUTY, AS USUAL... AND AS USUAL, HE ACTS LIKE I'M STILL A REGULAR, BUT I HAVEN'T BEEN HERE IN YEARS...

LEO, KID, YOU READ *FRANK* TODAY?

HAVEN'T SEEN THE PAPER

CHECK IT OUT. *CLASSIC.*

FRANK KAFKA, PRIVATE EYE... IT NEVER MAKES ANY GODDAMN SENSE.

by Jacob K.

FRANK KAFKA, PRIVATE EYE

THIS IS CRAZY... HOW AM I EVER GONNA FIND HER?

IT HAD TO BE A MISTAKE... A MISSING DAME, AND ME HER ONLY HOPE... BUT THE ONLY THING THEY GIVE ME IS HER NAME – H...

GLUG GLUG

... AND *ONE* PHOTO. IT'S GOT TO BE A MISTAKE, BUT THAT NEVER STOPPED ME BEFORE.

I DON'T GET IT.

YEAH.

SO, WHATTAYA KNOW, KIDDO? HOW'S *IVAN* HOLDIN' UP?

HELL ON WHEELS, 'TIL HE COLLAPSES.

I HEAR YA'... POOR OLD BASTARD.

THE UNDERTOW WAS OUR PLACE... THE *CRIMINAL ELEMENT*.

IT STARTED AS A SPEAKEASY, WAY BACK WHEN, BUT AFTER PROHIBITION, IT'D NEVER LOST ITS ROOTS.

IT WAS ALSO CONSIDERED A *SAFE ZONE*.

YOU COULD EVEN FIND *BLOOD ENEMIES* SIDE BY SIDE AT THE BAR MOST NIGHTS, AND ONLY ON *RARE OCCASIONS* DID ANYTHING GET OUT OF HAND.

THEN IT WAS USUALLY SOME *VIRGIN* WHO DIDN'T REALIZE WHERE THE HELL HE WAS.

OR THAT HE'D NEVER BE COMING BACK.

YOU SEEN *DONNIE* AROUND LATELY?

THE *SPAZ*?

YEAH.

NAH... HE COMES IN *DAYS*, I THINK... ON DENBY'S SHIFT.

HEARD HE'S BEEN WORKIN' THE *L* MOST NIGHTS... *CLEANIN' UP* WITH THAT SPAZ ACT.

HE REALLY *IS* EPILEPTIC, GNARLY.

PROB'LY WHY HE CAN FAKE IT SO GOOD.

I'LL CHECK OUT THE TRAINS...

TELL DENBY IF HE SEES HIM BEFORE I DO, TO GET IN TOUCH...

SURE, LEO.

YOU'RE TAKIN' *ORDERS* FROM THAT SON OF A BITCH?

YOU KNOW LESS THAN SHIT ABOUT HIM.

I KNOW WHAT I HEAR

YOU'RE ABOUT TO HEAR ME *CRACK* YOUR *SKULL*, YOU KEEP THAT UP.

HEY... I DIDN'T *MEAN NOTHIN'*... I WAS JUST TALKIN'...

I COULDN'T FIND FUCK-ALL ON YOUR SUPPOSED *SUPER-THIEF.*

JUST DIDN'T ADD UP, Y'KNOW? THAT HE WOULDN'T BE IN THE SYSTEM *AT ALL? NO WAY.*

JEFF. I *VOUCHED* FOR HIM, YOU DON'T NEED TO –

SO, I LOOKED A GENERATION *BACK,* AND BOY DID I GET A *HISTORY LESSON.*

YOU KNOW WHO THIS ASSHEAD'S DAD WAS? *TOMMY PATTERSON.*

NO WONDER HE CAN WORK A CROWD LIKE THAT. PROBABLY *GREW UP* DOIN' IT.

TOMMY AND HIS PARTNER *IVAN* RAN THE BEST PICKPOCKET CREW THIS CITY EVER SAW.

YEAH, I KNOW...

BUT IT SAYS HERE TOMMY *DIED* FIFTEEN YEARS AGO, SHANKED IN THE SHOWERS UPSTATE.

CONVICTED OF KILLIN' *TEEG LAWLESS.*

I KNOW ALL THAT, TOO. I KNEW HIS DAD.

WHAT'S YOUR *POINT?*

THAT EITHER THIS GUY'S AS GOOD AS YOU *SAID,* OR YOU BEEN *HOLDIN' BACK* ON ME.

WHICH IS IT?

IT'S *BOTH,* ACTUALLY... HE IS GOOD, THE BEST...

BUT THERE'S A *REASON* HE'S NEVER BEEN CAUGHT.

"LEO'S A **COWARD.**"

"HE DOESN'T JUST WALK AWAY FROM TROUBLE, HE **RUNS.**"

AND AS GOOD AS HE IS AT SEEING HOLES IN SECURITY AND MAPPING OUT SCORES...

...HE'S JUST THAT GOOD AT **SLIPPING AWAY,** TOO.

"THAT'S ONE OF THE REASONS WE NEED HIM, JEFF."

IF YOU GET MY MEANING.

SO THEN, YOU GUYS AREN'T EXACTLY FRIENDS?

LEO DOESN'T **HAVE** ANY FRIENDS...

"JUST THAT OLD MAN, **IVAN,** ALL SMACKED OUT AND LOSIN' HIS MIND.

"MAYBE A FEW OTHER GUYS, JUST AS **PATHETIC.**"

OH - OH GOD -

GGUUUGGG! GGUUGG!

THIS WAS DONNIE'S OPENING.

HE'D ATTRACT THE CROWD WITH THE SEIZURE...

GGGUUH! GGRRUUGGLLEE! UGGG!

SOMEONE DO -- WHAT'S HE --? JESUS! HE'S *CHOKING!*

...BUT THE REAL ACT WAS WHAT CAME NEXT.

MY GOD... ARE YOU OKAY?

I JUST... OH... WHAT'D I...? OH, NOT *AGAIN...*

LISTEN! I'M SORRY TO DISTURB YOU -- BUT -- BUT I'VE JUST HAD A *SEIZURE.*

AND I... I NEED TO GO TO THE *EMERGENCY ROOM.* I NEED... OH GOD...

I'M... I'M *HOMELESS* -- I DON'T HAVE INSURANCE... I DON'T --

THE HOSPITAL WON'T SEE ME, UNLESS I *PAY...* IT'S -- IT'S *95 DOLLARS* TO GET INTO THE ER...

CAN ANY OF YOU PLEASE *HELP ME?*

JUST -- PLEASE...?

AND THEY ALWAYS DID.

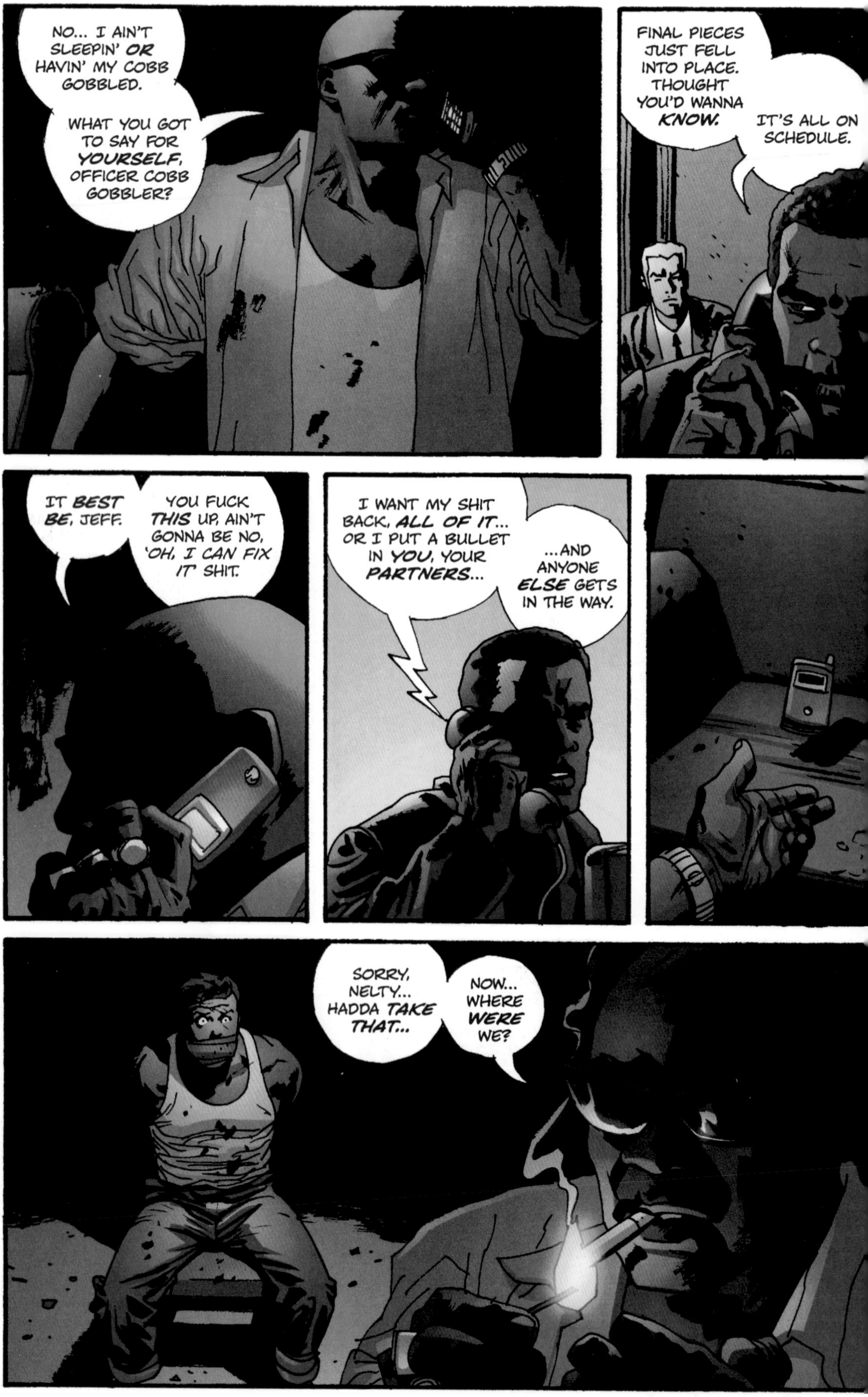

NO... I AIN'T SLEEPIN' OR HAVIN' MY COBB GOBBLED.
WHAT YOU GOT TO SAY FOR YOURSELF, OFFICER COBB GOBBLER?
FINAL PIECES JUST FELL INTO PLACE. THOUGHT YOU'D WANNA KNOW.
IT'S ALL ON SCHEDULE.
IT BEST BE, JEFF.
YOU FUCK THIS UP, AIN'T GONNA BE NO, 'OH, I CAN FIX IT' SHIT.
I WANT MY SHIT BACK, ALL OF IT... OR I PUT A BULLET IN YOU, YOUR PARTNERS...
...AND ANYONE ELSE GETS IN THE WAY.
SORRY, NELTY... HADDA TAKE THAT...
NOW... WHERE WERE WE?

Four Days Later...

I'M GONNA RUN AND GET MORE COFFEE.

WE'RE *WORKING*, SEYMOUR

S'WHY WE NEED IT.

WE'RE ON A CLOCK HERE.

IT TAKES *TWO SECONDS*.

GET OUT OF THAT SEAT AND I *WALK*, I SWEAR TO GOD.

ALL RIGHT... JESUS, LEO...

NOT LIKE WE HAVEN'T DONE THIS THE LAST *THREE* DAYS.

THEY ALWAYS TAKE THE *SAME ROUTE*.

AND THAT'S WHY *TODAY* IS DIFFERENT.

READ THE PAPER IF YOU'RE BORED.

I'M WORKING.

FINE.

FRANK KAFKA, PRIVATE EYE

by Ja[...]

I'D BEEN KNOCKING ON DOORS FOR DAYS, ASKING THE SAME QUESTIONS...

YOU KNOW A WOMAN NAME OF H? SHOULDER LENGTH BLACK HAIR, ABOUT YAY TALL?

THEN THE G-MEN SHOWED UP...

HELLO, FRANK... WHAT'S THIS I HEAR? YOU'RE ASKING AROUND 'BOUT SOME DEAD BROAD?

DEAD?

I NEVER SAID —

IT'S JUST LIKE LAST TIME, FRANK, YOU DON'T KNOW *WHAT* YOU'RE DOING, DO YOU?

ALL RIGHT, SEYMOUR, WE'RE ON...

...THE TARGET IS MOVING.

HAND ME YOUR CELL.

YOU DON'T *HAVE* A CELL-PHONE?

NO.

AND THAT'S ON *PRINCIPLE*, ISN'T IT? I MEAN, NOT LIKE YOU CAN'T *GRAB* ONE.

CELL-PHONES ARE ANNOYING.

NOW GIVE ME YOURS.

EVERY DAY AT 4:30 PM, THE VAN LEFT THE *EVIDENCE STORAGE FACILITY* AND DROVE TWO MILES TO THE DOWNTOWN COURTHOUSE.

THEY DELIVERED EVIDENCE FOR TRIAL THE NEXT DAY, WHICH NEEDED TO BE PROCESSED BEFORE IT COULD BE PRESENTED IN COURT.

SEYMOUR AND HIS CROOKED COP BUDDY JEFF WERE RIGHT...

THE TRANSPORT VAN WAS THE WEAK LINK.

BECAUSE NO ONE EVER KNEW WHAT IT WAS CARRYING, SO WHO WAS GOING TO TAKE DOWN A *POLICE TRANSPORT VEHICLE* ON THE OUTSIDE CHANCE OF A BIG SCORE?

NOT EVEN JUNKIES WERE THAT DESPERATE.

BUT WE HAD AN INSIDE MAN, AND KNEW THAT IN TWO DAYS THIS VAN WOULD BE CARRYING FIVE MILLION IN DIAMONDS.

BLOOD DIAMONDS, SMUGGLED FROM AFRICA, AND SEIZED IN A JEWELRY STORE RAID A FEW YEARS BACK.

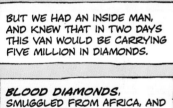

THE ACCUSED WERE FINALLY GETTING THEIR DAY IN COURT, AND THEIR LAWYER WAS SMART ENOUGH TO DEMAND ALL EVIDENCE BE PRESENT.

GREAT WAY TO INFLUENCE A JURY... SHOW THEM WHAT FIVE MIL IN GEMS LOOKS LIKE, AND ASK WHAT THEY'D DO IN THE DEFENDANT'S PLACE.

EXCEPT, THESE DIAMONDS WOULD NEVER MAKE IT TO THAT COURTHOUSE.

THAT'S *DONNIE*... WHAT'S HE DOING?

THE TRANSPORT VAN HAS A SET ROUTE.

SO... WHAT HAPPENS WHEN THEY CAN'T *TAKE IT?*

HEY! MOVE IT, ASSHOLE!

YOU MOVE IT!

GO AROUND!

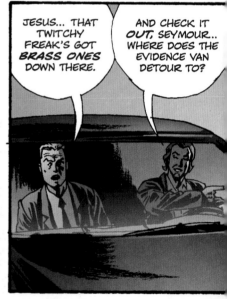

JESUS... THAT TWITCHY FREAK'S GOT *BRASS ONES* DOWN THERE.

AND CHECK IT *OUT,* SEYMOUR... WHERE DOES THE EVIDENCE VAN DETOUR TO?

JACKSON STREET TUNNEL... AND AT *RUSH HOUR,* PRACTICALLY.

YEP... CALL YOUR COP.

WE'VE GOT OUR *PLAN.*

WHO THE HELL IS **THIS?**

SOMEONE I **HIRED**, A PROFESSIONAL.

WHO THE FUCK ARE **THEY?**

MY PARTNERS.

BEST BACK-UP IN TOWN, IF THERE'S A **NEED**.

THERE **ISN'T**... GET THEM OUT OF HERE, **NOW**.

WHAT DID YOU JUST **SAY** TO ME?

SAY IT **AGAIN**, PUSSY!

JESUS! WHAT THE **FUCK?**

GUYS!

LISTEN UP. **SEYMOUR** MAY SAY YOU'RE IN CHARGE HERE...

...BUT I **FOUND** THIS JOB.

I CALL MY **OWN** SHOTS.

JEFF... TAKE IT EASY.

YOUR GUYS ARE **IN**. IT'S COOL.

RIGHT, LEO?

SURE... **WHATEVER**, BUT I'M PLACING THEM.

GO AHEAD, YOU'RE THE BIG **BRAIN**, RIGHT? THE MAN WITH THE **PLAN**?

I JUST WANNA KNOW WHO'S WATCHING MY BACK...

...IF THIS ALL GOES TITS UP.

IT **WON'T.** THE PLAN IS WATERTIGHT... AS LONG AS EVERYONE **FOLLOWS** IT.

THEN WHAT'S THIS SEYMOUR TELLS ME ABOUT SOME **NO GUNS** DEAL?

WE DON'T NEED THEM, SO WHY THE HELL SHOULD WE **BRING THEM?**

MAYBE BECAUSE WE'RE GOING UP AGAINST **ARMED COPS?**

AND YOU WANT US TO **SHOOT** THEM? AREN'T THEY YOUR **BROTHERS?**

LOOK, THIS IS **NOT** NEGOTIABLE.

THERE WILL BE **NO GUNS** ON THIS JOB, PERIOD. OR I **LEAVE** RIGHT NOW.

JESUS **FUCK**... SEYMOUR TOLD ME ABOUT YOU...

...BUT I DIDN'T THINK YOU REALLY HAD **NO NUTS** AT ALL.

AS A COP, YOU SHOULD KNOW THIS...

...BUT PRISONS ARE **FULL** OF ASSHOLES WHO VALUED THEIR OWN LIVES ONLY **SLIGHTLY** MORE THAN OTHER PEOPLE'S.

AND I'M NOT ENDING UP ON *DEATH ROW* BECAUSE SOME MORON LISTENED TO TOO MUCH *HIP HOP* GROWING UP.

IF THAT SAYS SOMETHING ABOUT ME, THEN *FINE*.

I'M HERE FOR *ONE REASON* ONLY... TO GET US ALL PAID.

NOW, DO YOU WANT TO *GET PAID?* OR AM I WASTING MY TIME?

I WANT TO GET PAID.

I JUST DON'T WANT TO HAVE MY ASS HANGIN' IN THE WIND.

IT *WON'T BE*, JEFF... JUST HEAR THE MAN OUT.

SO, WE ALL SETTLED ON THAT?

YEAH, *NO GUNS*... LET'S GO THROUGH THE RUNDOWN.

OKAY... FIRST, WE PAIR UP. GRETA AND *RED* WILL STAGE THE BREAKDOWN HERE...

JACKSON STREET TUNNEL

LEO, HOLD ON.

WHAT'S UP?

YOU *KNOW* THOSE BASTARDS ARE GOING TO TRY TO *SCREW US*, RIGHT?

THAT'S WHY HE'S BRINGING HIS WHOLE CREW IN.

YEAH, I *KNOW*. THEY'LL TRY TO GRAB THE DIAMONDS OR FUCK US OUT OF OUR END...

SOMETHING...

SO, WHAT DO WE *DO*?

WATCH OUR BACKS. UNLESS YOU WANT *OUT*?

NO. I *NEED* THIS.

MY ANGIE... SHE'S GOT *MEDICAL* STUFF. I CAN'T AFFORD IT...

MY MOM PITCHES IN WHAT SHE CAN, BABYSITS WHILE I TRY TO EARN, BUT...

...I'M *SINKING* HERE, LEO.

YEAH, I KNOW THE FEELING.

SO, WHAT'S OUR BACK-UP PLAN, THEN?

OUR BACK-UP PLAN?

SINCE WHEN DID YOU AND I BECOME A TEAM?

I'M THE *REASON* YOU'RE IN THIS, ASSHOLE, AND YOU KNOW IT.

DON'T *YOU* TRY AND FUCK ME OVER, TOO.

JUST FOLLOW THE PLAN, GRETA. I'M NOT GOING TO LET ANYTHING HAPPEN TO YOU, OR THE TAKE.

AND I'M JUST SUPPOSED TO TAKE THAT ON *FAITH* AND DO NOTHING?

LOOK, IF YOU WANT TO *HELP*, FIND OUT WHAT YOU CAN ABOUT JEFF AND HIS BOYS.

ONE CROOKED COP IS BAD ENOUGH, THREE COULD BE A *NIGHTMARE*.

BUT WITH THE JOB A DAY AWAY, I KNEW THERE WAS NO TIME LEFT TO DIG UP ANYTHING THAT'D MAKE A DIFFERENCE.

WE'D ALREADY ROLLED THE DICE, AND NOW WE HAD TO WAIT AND SEE HOW THEY CAME UP.

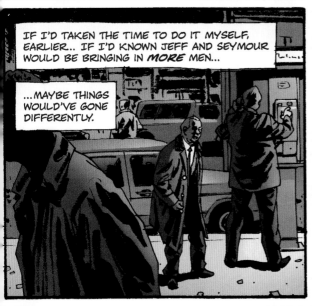

IF I'D TAKEN THE TIME TO DO IT MYSELF, EARLIER... IF I'D KNOWN JEFF AND SEYMOUR WOULD BE BRINGING IN *MORE* MEN...

...MAYBE THINGS WOULD'VE GONE DIFFERENTLY.

BUT I WAS DISTRACTED...

YOU *SURE*, GNARLY?

YEAH, NO PROBLEM... DON'T SWEAT IT.

I JUST NEED SOMEONE I CAN *TRUST*, Y'KNOW?

IT'LL BE A DAY, MAYBE TWO AT THE MOST, JUST IN CASE.

LOOK, DAGMAR LOVES IVAN, KIDDO, SO IT'S *NOT* A PROBLEM.

WELL, SHE HASN'T HAD TO DEAL WITH HIM *LATELY.*

JUST TELL HER TO *SLAP HIM* IF HE GETS OUTTA LINE.

BUT THANKS... HOPEFULLY AFTER THIS, I CAN GET HIM SOME *REAL* HELP...

WHAT ARE YOU *DOING?* STOP THAT.

BUT I THOUGHT WE WERE *WORKING?*

NOT ON THE *STREET.*

MA'AM... I THINK YOU DROPPED THIS.

OH, WELL THAT'S *MY...*

BUT HOW DID I --?

C'MON, IVAN ... WE'RE GONNA BE LATE.

GRETA CLAIMED THEY DIDN'T KNOW WHERE I LIVED, BUT IF *SHE* COULD FIND ME, IT DIDN'T FEEL SAFE ENOUGH.

AND I WASN'T LEAVING IVAN AND SOME DAY-NURSE AT THE MERCY OF WHOEVER CAME KNOCKING BECAUSE OF THIS JOB...

GIVING AWAY FREE MONEY...

YOU *NEVER* DO THAT... WHAT ARE WE, *MARKS?*

OF *COURSE* WE'RE NOT, BUT WE'RE ON A *MISSION* RIGHT NOW.

WHAT MISSION?

LOOKING FOR THE RICHEST MAN IN THE CITY.

SEBASTIAN HYDE? ON THE SUBWAY? I DON'T THINK SO, LEO.

OKAY, HOW ABOUT THE MAN WHO'S CARRYING THE MOST *CASH*, THEN? THINK YOU CAN SPOT *HIM?*

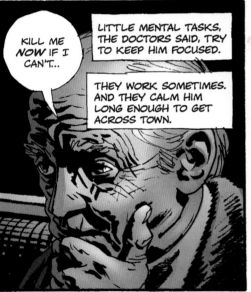

KILL ME *NOW* IF I CAN'T...

LITTLE MENTAL TASKS, THE DOCTORS SAID, TRY TO KEEP HIM FOCUSED.

THEY WORK SOMETIMES. AND THEY CALM HIM LONG ENOUGH TO GET ACROSS TOWN.

I WORRY MORE THAN I *SHOULD.* HE'S BEEN IN THE GAME SINCE HE WAS EIGHT, WEAVING THROUGH THE CROWDS ON THE CARNIVAL GROUNDS WHERE HE WAS RAISED.

BUT IF HE GOT CAUGHT, IT WOULD BE *WORSE* THAN A NIGHTMARE.

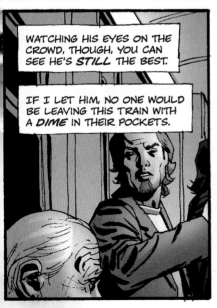

WATCHING HIS EYES ON THE CROWD, THOUGH, YOU CAN SEE HE'S *STILL* THE BEST.

IF I LET HIM, NO ONE WOULD BE LEAVING THIS TRAIN WITH A *DIME* IN THEIR POCKETS.

THOSE LITTLE SPARKS OF WHO HE *USED TO BE* MAKE ALL THE DIFFERENCE, BUT THEY CUT BOTH WAYS.

THIS IS OUR STOP, IVAN.

SURE, I... I ...

WHERE *ARE* WE...?

The Job

HERE'S THE THING... MOST HEISTS, EVEN GOOD ONES, ARE LIKE A *HOUSE OF CARDS*.

ONE MINOR DETAIL GOES WRONG, AND THEY COLLAPSE ALL AROUND YOU.

BUT I PLANNED FOR CONTINGENCIES. I *ORCHESTRATED*.

SO, MY SCORES BEGAN WITH A WELL-PLACED *DISTRACTION* FOR THE POLICE.

THIS TIME IT WAS DONNIE LEAVING A *SUSPICIOUS* PACKAGE IN A *JEWISH DELI* ON BROADWAY...

WE GOOD?

LET'S HIT IT...

THEY GOT A PICTURE OF THE MAYOR IN THERE, TAKIN' A BITE OUT OF A *PICKLE*.

I KNOW, THAT'S WHY I *CHOSE* IT. IT'S POPULAR WITH THE JERKS AT CITY HALL.

SO THE COPS'LL BE *EXTRA* CAREFUL AND WASTE *LOTS* OF MAN-POWER

GOTTA LOVE THE *WAR ON TERROR*, HUNH?

YEP... ONLY WINNERS ARE THE *THIEVES*.

SEYMOUR DID WHAT HE ALWAYS DID BEST, KEEPING THE CLOCK AND CALLING "GO" TIMES.

THE MOMENT THE EVIDENCE TRANSPORT TURNED ITS FIRST CORNER, HE WAS ON THE PHONE TO 911 REPORTING A BOMB THREAT AT THE DELI WE'D JUST LEFT.

BY THE TIME THEY GOT TO OUR *STAGED BREAKDOWN*, NEARLY EVERY SQUAD-CAR IN THE CITY WOULD BE RACING TO THE *OTHER SIDE* OF DOWNTOWN.

AND WHEN THEY PULLED INTO THE *JACKSON STREET TUNNEL*, THANKS TO CAREFUL TIMING AND SEYMOUR'S WATCHFUL EYE...

...THEY WERE PULLING IN *RIGHT BEHIND* ME AND DONNIE.

OKAY, HOW ABOUT THIS ONE...

YOU WILL DRINK THE BLACK SPERM OF MY VENGEANCE!

TOO EASY... *BEYOND THE VALLEY OF THE DOLLS.*

GRETA AND RED WOULD BE TWO OR THREE CARS BEHIND THEM, HAVING RELEASED THE JACK AND RACED BACK AROUND.

AND JEFF'S PARTNERS WERE CREATING A *TRAFFIC JAM* TWENTY YARDS AHEAD...

HNNK

BLLEEP

HOONK

BREEET

...NEXT TO AN *ABANDONED* CAR THAT DONNIE AND I PLACED THIRTY MINUTES EARLIER

OUT OF GAS PLEASE DON'T TOW

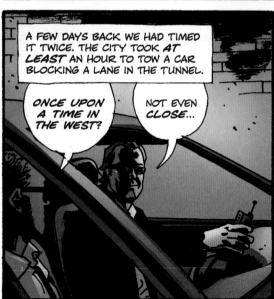

A FEW DAYS BACK WE HAD TIMED IT TWICE. THE CITY TOOK *AT LEAST* AN HOUR TO TOW A CAR BLOCKING A LANE IN THE TUNNEL.

ONCE UPON A TIME IN THE WEST?

NOT EVEN *CLOSE*...

AND WITH SEYMOUR AND JEFF IN THE GETAWAY CAR NEARBY, MONITORING POLICE TRAFFIC...

ALL CLEAR, LEO. THEY JUST CORDONED OFF *SIX BLOCKS* OF BROADWAY, *BOMB SQUAD* AND EVERYTHING.

RIGHT.

...IT WAS TIME TO MOVE.

HELP ME!

SOMETHING'S *WRONG!* MY FRIEND IS *DYING!*

GGUUHHH - GUUH! GLLUUHH!

HEY! HEY!

YOU'RE A *COP!* YOU KNOW *CPR!* HELP HIM!

JESUS... *LOOK* AT THAT FUCKIN' GUY...

JUST GO... WE'RE STUCK IN TRAFFIC ANYWAY.

THE *FUCK* IS HIS PROBLEM?

EVERYONE STARTED HONKING THEIR *HORNS* AND HE JUST *FREAKED OUT.*

JESUS... YOU GOTTA MAKE SURE HE AIN'T EATIN' HIS OWN TONGUE, AN' THEN...

GGLLLUUHH! GGUU!

BBZZZZZRRRTTT

AAAAHHH!

I NEED **BACK-UP**, NOW! JACKSON STREET TUNNEL - **OFFICER DOWN!**

SONS OF BITCHES! YOU --

KKRRRZZZZKKK

AAAAHHHH!

CATCH.

WE'RE IN. WHAT'S OUR **TIME** LIKE?

SQUAD CARS'RE ON THE WAY, BUT THEY'RE TWO MINUTES OUT, AT LEAST.

YOU GOT THE **EVIDENCE** NUMBER? YOU'RE LOOKING FOR A **METAL BRIEFCASE.**

YEAH. JUST GIMME A SECOND...

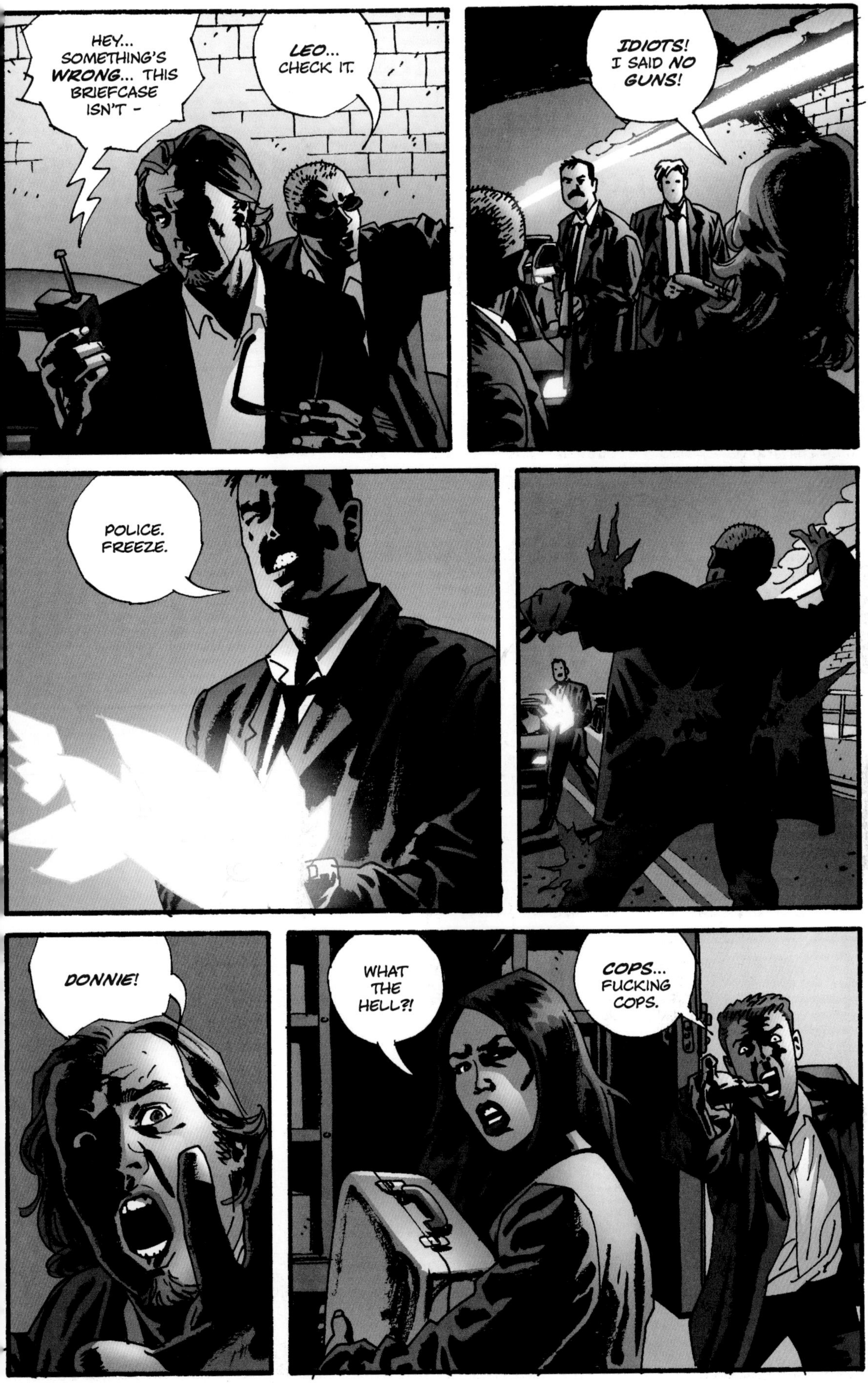

HEY... SOMETHING'S WRONG... THIS BRIEFCASE ISN'T -
LEO... CHECK IT.
IDIOTS! I SAID NO GUNS!
POLICE. FREEZE.
DONNIE!
WHAT THE HELL?!
COPS... FUCKING COPS.

POLICE! DROP YOUR WEAPONS!

AHH!

FUCK!

SUDDENLY, OUR GETAWAY ROUTE IS CUT-OFF BY COPS RESPONDING TO AN *OFFICER DOWN* CALL.

COPS WHO *SHOULD* HAVE BEEN AT THE BOMB THREAT THAT SEYMOUR HAD CLEARLY *NOT* CALLED IN.

I'D UNDERESTIMATED HIM AND JEFF.

I THOUGHT THEY'D TRY TO SCREW US *AFTER* THE JOB, NOT *DURING*.

DAMN IT...

HEY...COP...

WE NEED TO GO. CAN YOU **MOVE?**

DOES... **BLEEDING** COUNT...?

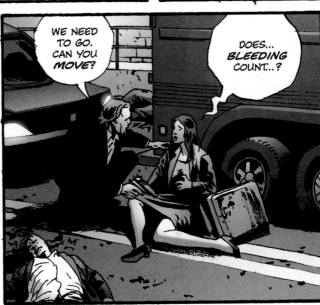

COME ON... YOU CAN DO IT.

AH! JESUS! OW! OW!

THEY'VE GOT THE **CASE!**

SHOOT THEM!

FREEZE!

SCREW YOU.

FUCK!

WHAT ARE YOU DOING?!

THEY'RE GETTING AWAY!

OUT OF GAS PLEASE DON'T TOU

LUCKY FOR ME, I'D **ALWAYS** HAD MY OWN WAY OUT OF HERE.

IT WAS JUST ABOUT THE ONLY RULE I **HADN'T** BROKEN -- NEVER GO INTO A SCORE WITH ONLY ONE EXIT.

AND THERE WAS A REASON I'D CHOSEN THIS EXACT MODEL OF CAR

BECAUSE IT COULD GO ON ROADS THE POLICE COULDN'T FOLLOW ME DOWN.

SHOP-FILLED ALLEYWAYS MEANT FOR WALKING, NOT DRIVING.

BUT THE HELL WITH THAT. THOSE WERE SOMEONE ELSE'S RULES.

OWW... BLEEDING PRETTY BAD... LEO...

JESUS... IT HURTS...

JUST HANG ON... YOU'RE GOING TO BE FINE...

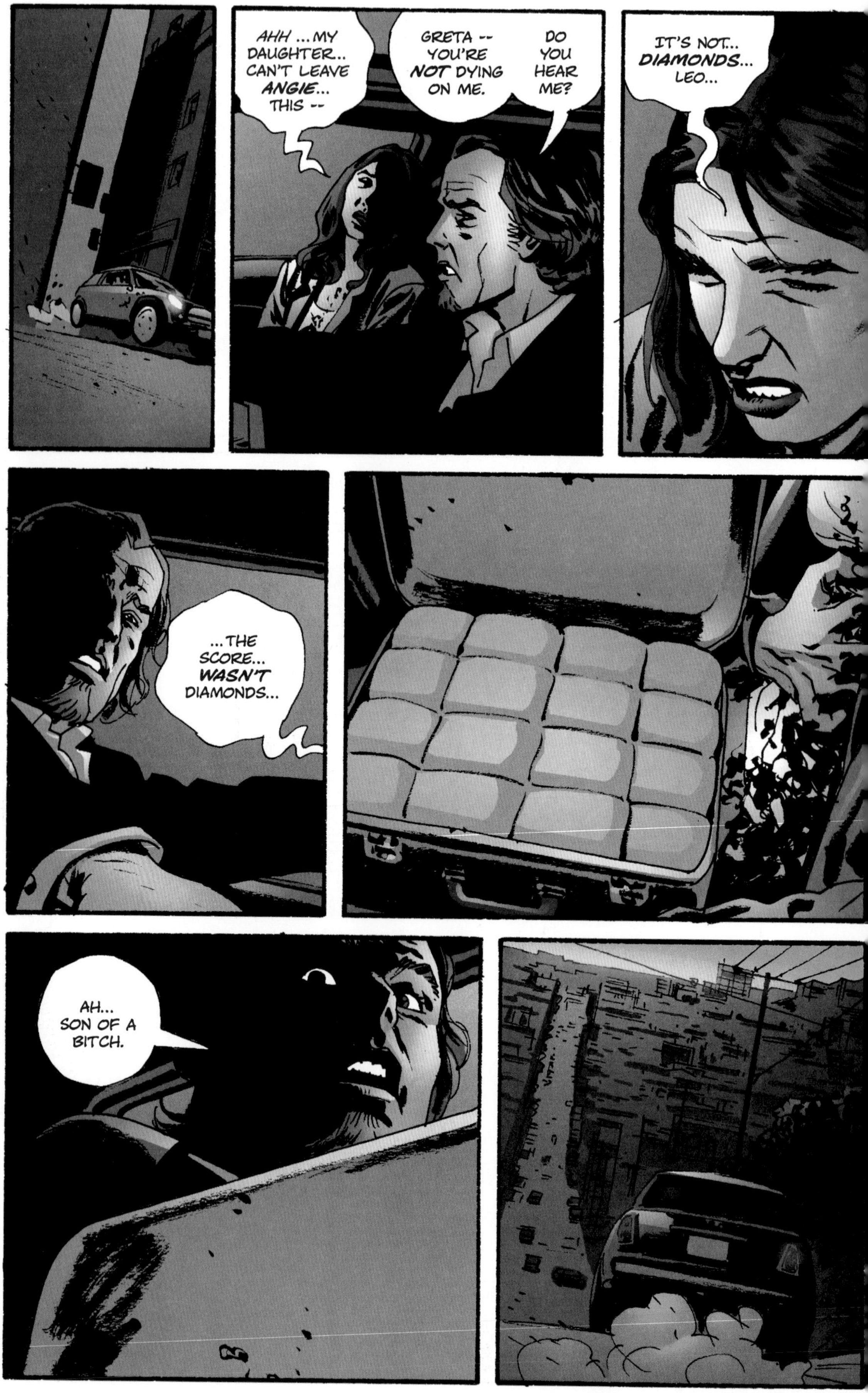

AHH ... MY DAUGHTER.. CAN'T LEAVE ANGIE... THIS --
GRETA -- YOU'RE NOT DYING ON ME.
DO YOU HEAR ME?
IT'S NOT... DIAMONDS... LEO...
...THE SCORE... WASN'T DIAMONDS...
AH... SON OF A BITCH.

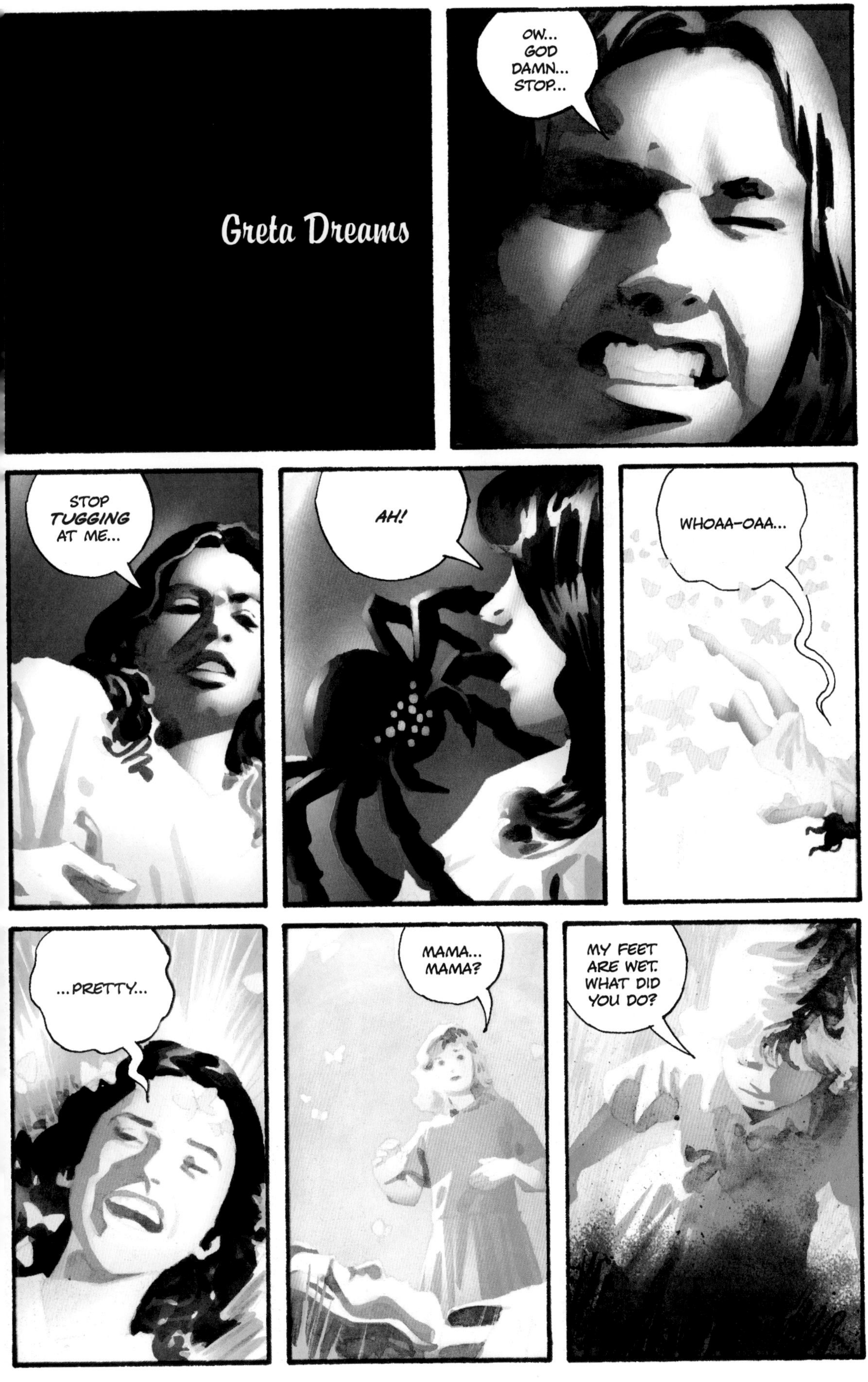
Greta Dreams
OW... GOD DAMN... STOP...
STOP *TUGGING* AT ME...
AH!
WHOAA-OAA...
...PRETTY...
MAMA... MAMA?
MY FEET ARE WET. WHAT DID YOU DO?

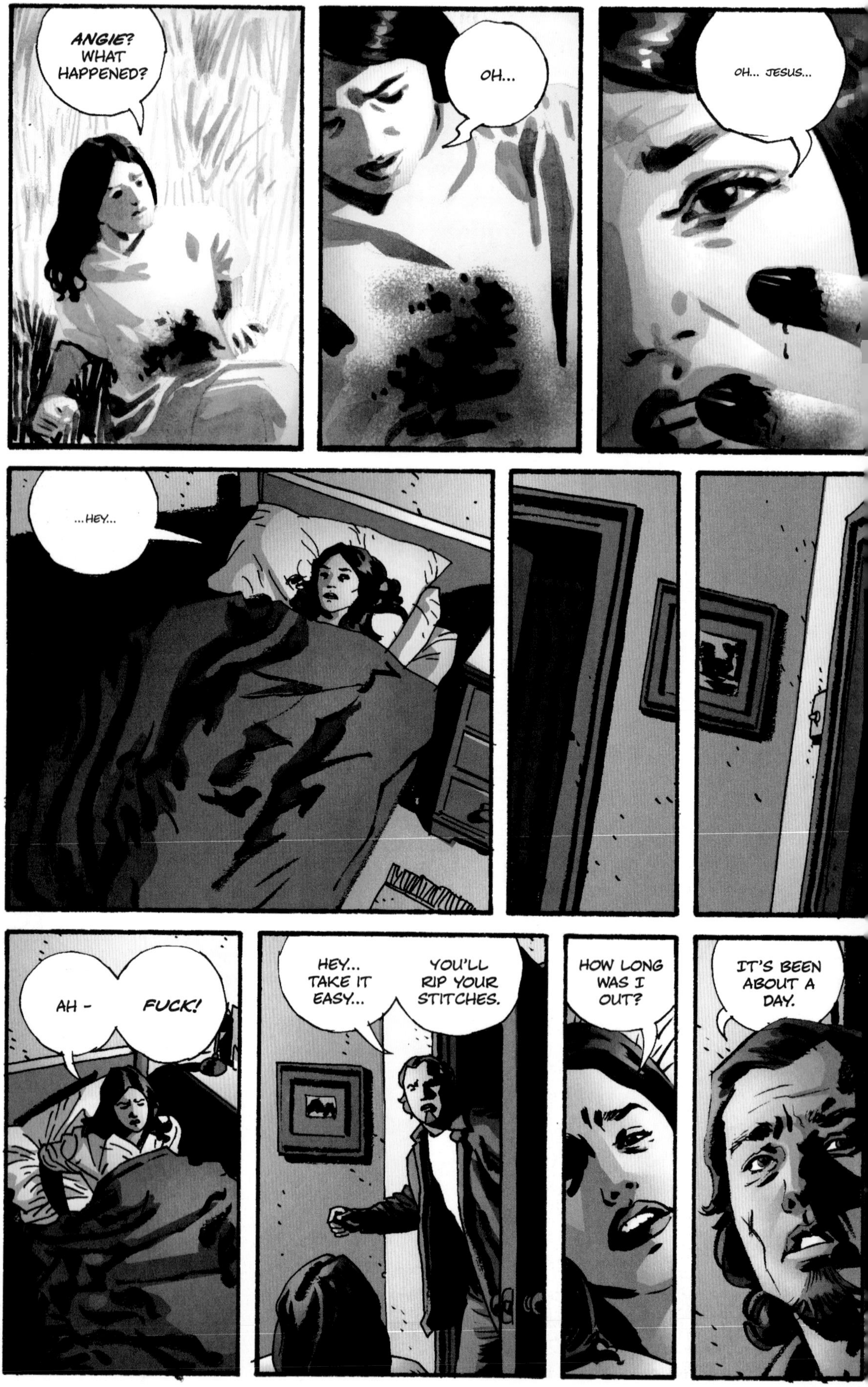

ANGIE? WHAT HAPPENED?
OH...
OH... JESUS...
...HEY...
AH -
FUCK!
HEY... TAKE IT EASY...
YOU'LL RIP YOUR STITCHES.
HOW LONG WAS I OUT?
IT'S BEEN ABOUT A DAY.

THERE WAS SOME KIND OF... SURGERY...?

YEAH. AT A FRIEND OF THE FAMILY'S NEARBY...

GUY WAS A *FIELD SURGEON* IN VIETNAM...

SAID HE'D SEEN LOTS OF WORSE BULLET WOUNDS THAN YOURS.

HE *DOPED* ME UP...

NOT A LOT OF CHOICE ON THAT, SORRY. HE HAD TO OPERATE, AND YOU WERE SCREAMING.

I'LL LIVE.

YEAH, YOU WILL.

I NEED TO CALL MY MOM... MAKE SURE ANGIE'S OKAY...

THEY DON'T KNOW WHERE I AM...

I CAN'T LET YOU DO THAT RIGHT NOW.

IT ISN'T *SAFE.*

KRNNCH

...FUCKIN'... AH...

LEAVE HIM *ALONE,* ROY! *GOD DAMN IT!*

IT'S NOT HIS *FAULT!*

MARVIN. HELP THE POLICEMAN REMEMBER WHO HE TALKIN' TO...

KRAK

FUCK YOU!

SMAK

OKAY... DAMN IT... *BUT WE STILL* GOT YOUR MAN DELRON A *WALK.*

WE MAY'VE LOST THE SUITCASE, BUT IT DIDN'T SHOW UP IN *COURT*... DID IT?

I AIN'T HAVIN' YOU BEAT ON FOR *THAT* SHIT, JEFFIE BOY...

BUT NO ONE CALLS ME ROY NO MORE.

NAME BE *ROY-L.T.*

AN' I'M 'ONNA BE THE *KING* A'THIS TOWN.

AN' THE KING *DON'T* ALLOW FAILURE...

LARRY!

YOU **MOTHERFUCKER!** YOU DIDN'T HAVE TO **DO THAT!**

THAT'S RIGHT, I DIDN'T **HAVE** TO, BUT I DID IT ANYWAY...

KNOW WHAT **ELSE** I DON'T HAVE'TA DO?

LET **YOUR** BLACK COP-ASS WALK OUTTA HERE.

I CAN GET IT BACK. I CAN FIND THE GUY...

I **KNEW** YOU'D BE SAYIN' THAT.

BUT SEE, YOU BEEN FUCKIN' UP LEFT AN' RIGHT, JEFF... SO, LIKE, MY **TRUST** HAS ISSUES AN' SHIT.

BUT YOU **DID** GET MY LIEUTENANT OUT OF A SPOT...

SPOT HE SHOULD'A BEEN KEPT CLEAR OF IN THE **FIRST PLACE**, BUT... I'LL GIVE YOU YOUR LIFE FOR THAT.

NOW LET'S YOU AN' HIM GO FIND ME MY MOTHERFUCKIN' **CHIBA.**

NO, **WHAT?** YOU WANT ME TO WORK WITH **DELRON?**

THAT'S **RIGHT**, OFFICER HE BE MY EYES. SO DON'T LET HIM SEE YOU FUCKIN' UP...

OR YOU BE JUST LIKE YOUR PARTNER..

...DEAD DEAD DEAD.

BOY, YOU REALLY DON'T LISTEN TO DOCTOR'S ORDERS, DO YOU?

I'VE BEEN LYIN' ON MY ASS FOR *TWO DAYS*, DAMN IT.

I NEED TO CALL MY MOM. LET HER KNOW I'M NOT DEAD, OR *WORSE*...

SHE *HAS* TO HAVE SEEN NEWS OF THE *HEIST*, AND IF THERE'S A SKETCH OF A WOMAN...

THERE *ISN'T*.

IT'S BEEN ON THE NEWS, BUT THEY'RE KEEPING THE DETAILS VAGUE...

AND YOU AND I *HAVEN'T* BEEN FINGERED YET.

BECAUSE WE HAVE THE SCORE.

YEP. WE HAVE WHAT THEY WANT.

SO, WHERE ARE WE? WHAT *IS* THIS PLACE?

SOMEPLACE *SAFE* TO WAIT OUT THE *STORM*.

THANKS FOR BEING VAGUE. WHERE'S THE PHONE?

GRETA... SIT DOWN. YOU'RE NOT THINKING CLEARLY.

AS FAR AS JEFF AND SEYMOUR *KNOW*, YOU MIGHT BE *DEAD*.

WHEN I *DRAGGED* YOU OUT OF THERE, YOU WERE LEAKING *A LOT* OF BLOOD...

SO RIGHT NOW, YOUR DAUGHTER IS OF *NO INTEREST* TO THEM. YOU *DON'T* WANNA CHANGE THAT.

FUCK... WE REALLY STEPPED IN IT THIS TIME, DIDN'T WE?

LOOK, JUST BE SMART AND SIT TIGHT HERE. I'VE GOTTA GO OUT FOR A WHILE.

WHERE'RE YOU GOING?

TO COVER *MY OWN* ASS.

CAN YOU PICK ME UP SOME *CIGARETTES*, AT LEAST?

THERE WAS NO TWO WAYS ABOUT IT. I HAD BLOWN IT. I KNEW THERE WAS SOMETHING OFF ABOUT THIS JOB, BUT I HAD GONE AHEAD WITH IT ANYWAY.

I HADN'T THOUGHT FAR ENOUGH AHEAD, HADN'T PLANNED FOR ALL THE ANGLES. THE THINGS I WAS SUPPOSED TO BE SO GOOD AT.

--STILL **NO LEADS** IN THE DARING DAYTIME ROBBERY OF A POLICE EVIDENCE VAN THAT LEFT A POLICE OFFICER DEAD EARLIER THIS WEEK.

WHILE AUTHORITIES REMAIN TIGHT-LIPPED, SOURCES INDICATE THAT AMONG ITEMS TAKEN IN THE HEIST...

...WAS EVIDENCE FROM A HIGH-PROFILE **DRUG-TRAFFIC KING** CASE.

NO SHIT, SHERLOCK.

I CHECKED THE COURT DOCKET, AND SAW THE DIAMOND SMUGGLING CASE WAS SET FOR TRIAL...

--then I heard him tell the singer, there's a song my momma sung...

...BUT I DIDN'T TRY TO FIND OUT **WHO ELSE** WAS IN COURT THAT DAY.

...won't you sing it once, before we move along...

INTERSTATE 99

I TRUSTED THAT **GREED** WAS THE PRIME MOTIVATOR, WHEN IT WAS ONLY ONE OF THEM.

I READ THE WHOLE SITUATION WRONG. I STILL DIDN'T UNDERSTAND **HOW**, BUT I HAD.

City
79 MILES

REST AREA

I'D GOTTEN DONNIE AND RED KILLED... AND MAYBE GRETA AND ME, TOO.

MAYBE NONE OF US WOULD GET OUT OF THIS ALIVE.

THANKS FOR COMING. YOU WEREN'T FOLLOWED?

NOTHING I COULD SPOT.

YOU OKAY, KIDDO?

I'VE SEEN BETTER WEEKS. HOW WAS *HE*?

NOT TOO BAD, LONG AS HE'S HIGH.

SO, WHAT DO YOU NEED?

YOU'VE ALREADY DONE TOO MUCH. I DON'T WANT TO GET YOU IN *MY* TROUBLE, GNARLY.

IT'S NO TROUBLE FOR ME, LEO.

THERE *IS* ONE THING... IF YOU COULD LEAK WORD THAT GRETA DIDN'T MAKE IT...

MIGHT TAKE THE *PRESSURE* OFF A BIT...

OKAY... I'LL PUT IT IN THE RIGHT EARS.

AND YOU CALL IF YOU NEED *ANYTHING*.

WHAT I **NEEDED** WAS A TIME MACHINE, TO GO BACK AND NOT MAKE ALL THE SAME MISTAKES OVER AGAIN...

...BUT I'D PROBABLY MAKE NEW ONES THAT WERE JUST AS BAD.

HEY LEO... THERE'S A **GIRL** SLEEPIN' ON THE COUCH. A HOT ONE.

YOU GETTIN' SOME **NOOKIE** OUT HERE?

M'NOT ASLEEP... I'M –

OW!

FUCK!

AND SHE'S GOT **MY** KINDA MANNERS.

YOU MUST BE **IVAN**.

IS THIS MY NEW HANDLER?

NO, SHE'S NOT... SO GET **HANDLING** OFF YOUR BRAIN.

HE BEATS ME.

BUT NO ONE'LL *LISTEN* BECAUSE I'VE GOT ALZHEIMER'S.

OH, YOU POOR THING...

DO *NOT* HUMOR HIM. PLEASE.

AND IVAN, STOP TELLING PEOPLE THAT... IT *ISN'T* FUNNY.

SHE LIKED IT.

SURE, BUT SHE'S RECOVERING FROM A GUNSHOT...

NOW, LET'S GET YOU TO BED.

OKAY, OKAY... YOU GOT MY KIT?

DON'T I ALWAYS?

HERE.

OH... THANKS.

IS THAT YOUR PARENTS?

YEAH, THIS WAS MY GRANDFATHER'S FARM... HE PUT IT INTO A TRUST FOR MY MOM, CAUSE HE DIDN'T WANT MY DAD'S NAME ON IT.

SO IT'S MY HOME AWAY, WHEN I NEED ONE.

HOW OFTEN IS THAT?

I HAVEN'T BEEN HERE SINCE RIGHT AFTER THE SALT BAY JOB.

RIGHT...

SO, IVAN... YOU JUST SHOT HIM UP, RIGHT?

DON'T ASK ME TO EXPLAIN.

I DON'T NEED TO, BUT... I CAN'T HAVE THAT AROUND ME.

NOT *HIS* STUFF, OR THE SHIT THAT WAS IN THAT BRIEFCASE...

JUST... HIDE THEM SOMEPLACE *GOOD*, PLEASE.

SURE, GRETA...

HOW MUCH WAS THERE IN THAT CASE, ANYWAY?

YOU DON'T WANT TO KNOW.

HOW MUCH?

THIRTY TWO KILOS.

JESUS FUCKING CHRIST. I *KNEW* IT...

THE *MINUTE* I GRABBED THAT SUITCASE, I WAS JUST LIKE ... THIS THING WEIGHS *WAY TOO MUCH*...

WHAT'S A KILO OF SMACK GO FOR THESE DAYS? ANY IDEA?

HARD TO *SAY*... DEPENDS ON PURITY. BUT THE AVERAGE IS ABOUT THIRTY GRAND, I THINK.

THAT'S OVER 900 THOUSAND DOLLARS.

A LOT MORE ONCE IT GETS TO THE *STREET*.

FUCK.

THIS *ISN'T* JUST GONNA BLOW OVER, IS IT?

NO... WE MAY BE HERE A WHILE...

...BUT *EVERYTHING* BLOWS OVER EVENTUALLY.

YEAH, WELL YOU *BETTER* BE LOOKING, SEYMOUR...

I GOT A WEEK OFF CAUSE TOM GOT KILLED IN THE ROBBERY...

BUT THE BOSSES ARE BUGGING ME ABOUT LARRY... WANNA HEAR FROM HIM.

SO I CAN'T STAY OFF THEIR RADAR FOR MUCH LONGER

I KNOW... BUT *YOU* GET PAID WHEN ROY-L GETS HIS SHIT.

DO NOT BE *WHININ'* AT ME... I DON'T CARE ABOUT YOUR PROBLEMS.

YOU KNOW WHO I'M *WORKIN' WITH* ON THIS?

YEAH, AN' HE'S A *FUCKIN'* PSYCHO.

SO, FIND ME AN *ADDRESS*... AND SOON.

LATER BABY...

BYE DELRON... YOU COME ON BACK SOON.

YOU KEEP THAT ASS *TIGHT*, AN' I WILL.

AN' HOW ABOUT YOUR TIGHT ASS, JEFFY?

FUCK YOUR MOTHER

SHIT... NOT EVEN WITH *YOUR* COCK.

LET'S ROLL.

SEE, YOU JUST AIM AND BREATH, AND SQUEEZE.

YOU'RE SERIOUSLY *OKAY* FOR THIS?

FEELS LIKE SOMEONE'S PINCHING ME TOGETHER INSIDE, BUT IT'S NOT TOO BAD.

TRY GIVING *BIRTH* SOME TIME.

JUST BEING *BORN* WAS ENOUGH STRAIN FOR ME, THANKS.

SO, YOU GONNA SHOOT THAT, OR JUST PLAY WITH IT?

I *HAVE* FIRED A GUN BEFORE.

YEAH, I SAW. YOU *MISSED* A GUY TEN FEET AWAY.

SO HERE WE ARE.

PATHETIC. YOU'D THINK A GUY THAT GOOD WITH HIS HANDS COULD DO THIS.

FUCK YOU, THAT WAS *CLOSE*.

CLOSE...

MAYBE WE SHOULD GET YOU A *SAWED-OFF*...

THEY PROBABLY AREN'T *TOO HARD* TO FIND OUT HERE.

THERE'S ONE IN THE KITCHEN CUPBOARD, ACTUALLY. BUT NO SHELLS.

LET'S GET SOME, THEN.

WE'VE BEEN COOPED-UP FOR DAYS HERE ANYWAY...

WILL IVAN BE OKAY IF WE GO TO TOWN FOR A WHILE?

YEAH, HE'LL BE *OUT* FOR A WHILE AFTER HIS... YOU KNOW.

WHEN IS THAT?

SOONISH.

GREAT, IS THERE A *DINER*? I COULD KILL FOR SOME PIE...

WE COULD JUST GIVE IT BACK...

SURE, IF WE KNEW *WHOSE* PROPERTY IT WAS IN THE FIRST PLACE...

COULDN'T BE TOO HARD TO FIND OUT.

BUT THEN THERE'S THE WHOLE 'NOT-GETTING-KILLED' ANGLE.

PEOPLE LIKE THIS... NOT EXACTLY THE KIND I LIKE TO DEAL WITH.

NO RESPECT FOR ANYTHING... NO *RULES*.

YEAH, THAT SOUNDS LIKE *MOST* OF THE DRUG DEALERS I EVER KNEW...

THE WAY IT WAS PACKAGED, I'VE ONLY SEEN BRICKS LIKE THAT A FEW TIMES.

IT'S GOTTA BE SOMEONE *MAJOR*... A FIRST SHIPMENT FROM A NEW SOURCE OR SOMETHING.

AND IT'S PROBABLY *UNCUT*, WHICH MAKES IT EVEN *MORE* VALUABLE.

DAMN... THERE'S GOTTA BE A WAY TO GET *PAID* FOR THIS AND STILL WALK AWAY...

SERIOUSLY?

I DON'T WORK FOR FREE. NOT IF I DON'T HAVE TO.

IS THAT ONE OF YOUR RULES?

DO **NOT** MOCK THE RULES. YOU'RE ONLY **HERE** BECAUSE OF THEM.

BUT NO, IT'S MORE LIKE **IVAN'S** LAW...

YOU NEVER GIVE AWAY FREE MONEY.

HE'S A SWEET OLD GUY... BUT Y'KNOW HE TRIED TO GRAB MY **ASS** AT BREAKFAST YESTERDAY MORNING?

I'M SHOCKED...

BASTARD.

I OWE HIM A LOT... MORE THAN I CAN GIVE HIM.

HE KEPT ME OUT OF THE **SYSTEM**, AFTER MY DAD WENT **UPSTATE**.

IS THAT WHEN HE TAUGHT YOU WHAT YOU DO?

NO, I PICKED THAT UP FROM HIM AND DAD WHEN I WAS LITTLE...

THINK I WAS **EIGHT** WHEN I DID MY FIRST **GRAB** IN A CROWD.

JESUS... WHAT KIND OF –

HEY, GIRL...

...AIN'T SEEN *YOU* AROUND HERE BEFORE.

HOW 'BOUT YOU DITCH THE *TROUSER PIRATE* AND HAVE A DRINK WITH SOME MEN?

LET ME KNOW IF YOU *SEE* ANY AND I WILL.

GRETA...

GONNA LET YOUR *WOMAN* TALK FOR YOU, BOY?

LOOK, WE'RE JUST TRYING TO MIND OUR OWN BUSINESS, NOT START ANY *TROUBLE*...

CHRIST... WHAT A FUCKIN' WASTE...

WOW. GENUINE BUMPKINS...

WE BETTER HEAD BACK.

DAMN IT, THE FEED STORE'S CLOSED AND WE FORGOT THE SHOTGUN SHELLS...

YOU WEREN'T THE *SLIGHTEST BIT* AFRAID OF THOSE GUYS... WERE YOU?

THOSE FOOLS? NO.

BUT YOU BACKED RIGHT DOWN...

YEAH.

WHY?

BECAUSE I'M AFRAID OF *OTHER THINGS*... I GUESS.

VIOLENCE JUST... IT'S GOT A RIPPLE EFFECT. *YOU* KNOW THAT.

AND I TRY NOT TO CAUSE ANY RIPPLES...

MY EGO CAN TAKE A FEW *MORONS* THINKING THEY SCARED ME.

YOU'RE DIFFERENT THAN I ALWAYS *THOUGHT* YOU WERE.

PEOPLE *USUALLY* ARE...

YEAH, BUT USUALLY IT'S A *DISAPPOINTMENT.*

AAHHH... OW...

DAMN... THAT'S UGLY.

HEY, IVAN'S DOWN FOR THE COUNT, IF YOU WANNA WATCH –

HEY!

SHIT. SORRY... FUCK. I DIDN'T –

NO. IT'S OKAY...

...I WAS JUST TRYING TO DECIDE IF MY NEW *SCAR* WAS TOO HIDEOUS TO SHOW YOU.

NO... SCARS JUST MAKE YOUR BODY *MORE BEAUTIFUL*, GRETA.

THE ONLY ONES I WORRY ABOUT ARE ON THE *INSIDE*.

YOU'RE DIFFERENT.

SHE'S DIFFERENT, NOT ME... FRAGILE AND TOUGH ALL AT ONCE.

BUT HER TOUCH IS SO SOFT, I ALMOST MELT...

...AND THOUGHTS OF OUR PROBLEMS MELT WITH ME.

AT SOME POINT BEFORE WE DRIFT OFF, SHE WHISPERS, "TELL ME IT'S GOING TO BE OKAY."

AND I PROMISE HER IT WILL BE.

I PROMISE TO FIND US A WAY OUT.

AND AT THE TIME, I EVEN THINK I MEAN IT.

TOMMY... I NEED TO FIX...

WHERE ARE YOU?

TOMMY?

KNOW YOU'VE GOT *SOMETHING* STASHED AROUND HERE...

BINGO.

AND THEY SAY I'M LOSING IT.

WHOA... JACKPOT.

THIS IS A MISTAKE. WE DON'T EVEN KNOW IF SHE'S ALIVE OR DEAD...

JUST GET OUT YOUR FUCKIN' *BADGE* AND FOLLOW MY LEAD.

ROY-L'S GETTIN' SICK OF WAITIN' SO IT'S TIME TO SHAKE THE TREES.

THEY MIGHT NOT EVEN BE *HOME.*

THINK I BEEN ARRESTED ENOUGH TIMES TO KNOW *WHY* COPS SHOW UP AT THE ASS CRACK OF DAWN...

EVERYONE'S HOME.

WHAT IS THE *MEANING* OF THIS?

DO YOU KNOW WHAT *TIME* IT IS?

YES WE *DO,* MA'AM. WE'RE POLICE.

OH...

NEED TO SPEAK TO YOU ABOUT YOUR *DAUGHTER,* GRETA.

COULD WE COME INSIDE?

I'M NOT MUCH OF A SLEEPER, USUALLY, WHICH I ALWAYS FIGURED WAS BECAUSE I HAD TOO MUCH ON MY MIND...

BUT I HADN'T HAD *THIS* MUCH ON MY MIND IN YEARS, AND SOMEHOW, I WAS SLEEPING. HEAVY SLEEP.

ONE MINUTE I'M LYING WITH GRETA IN THE DARK...

...AND THE NEXT THING I KNOW, IT'S NOON.

FOR A SECOND, IT ALMOST FEELS LIKE A MIRACLE.

SHE HAD MADE MY MIND *QUIET*.

HOW HAD SHE DONE THAT?

RIGHT THEN, I KNEW *WHATEVER* WAS GOING ON, IT WAS ABOUT MORE THAN SURVIVAL.

AND I COULDN'T EVEN REMEMBER WHAT ANYTHING BEYOND THAT FELT LIKE ANYMORE.

IF ONLY I HADN'T OPENED THE DOOR AND LEFT THAT ROOM.

IVAN?

IF ONLY I COULD HAVE STAYED THERE FOREVER...

...AND KEPT THE WORLD OUT.

HEY, *OLD MAN?*

WHAT THE --

-- FUCK

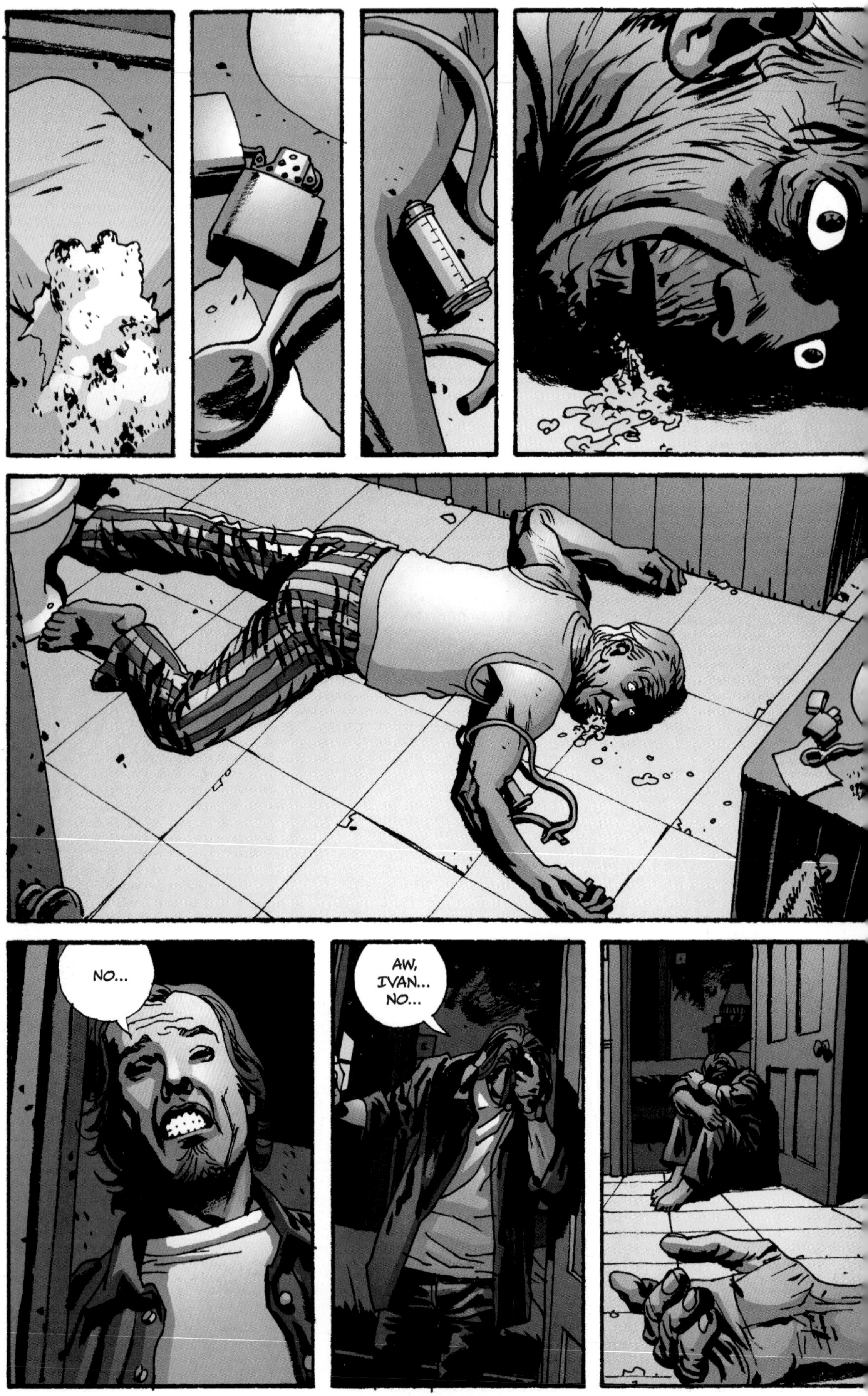
NO...
AW, IVAN... NO...

OH JESUS...

... LEO...

I OVERSLEPT...

...SO HE WENT LOOKING FOR SOMETHING TO SHOOT UP.

NO, LISTEN TO ME... YOU DID **NOT** DO THIS.

DIDN'T I?

I BROUGHT HIM HERE TO KEEP HIM SAFE...

...AND THEN I LEFT HIM ALONE WITH A BUNCH OF **UNCUT** HEROIN.

NO. YOU HID IT.

FROM **YOU.**

HE KNOWS THIS HOUSE.

KNEW... **KNEW** THIS HOUSE.

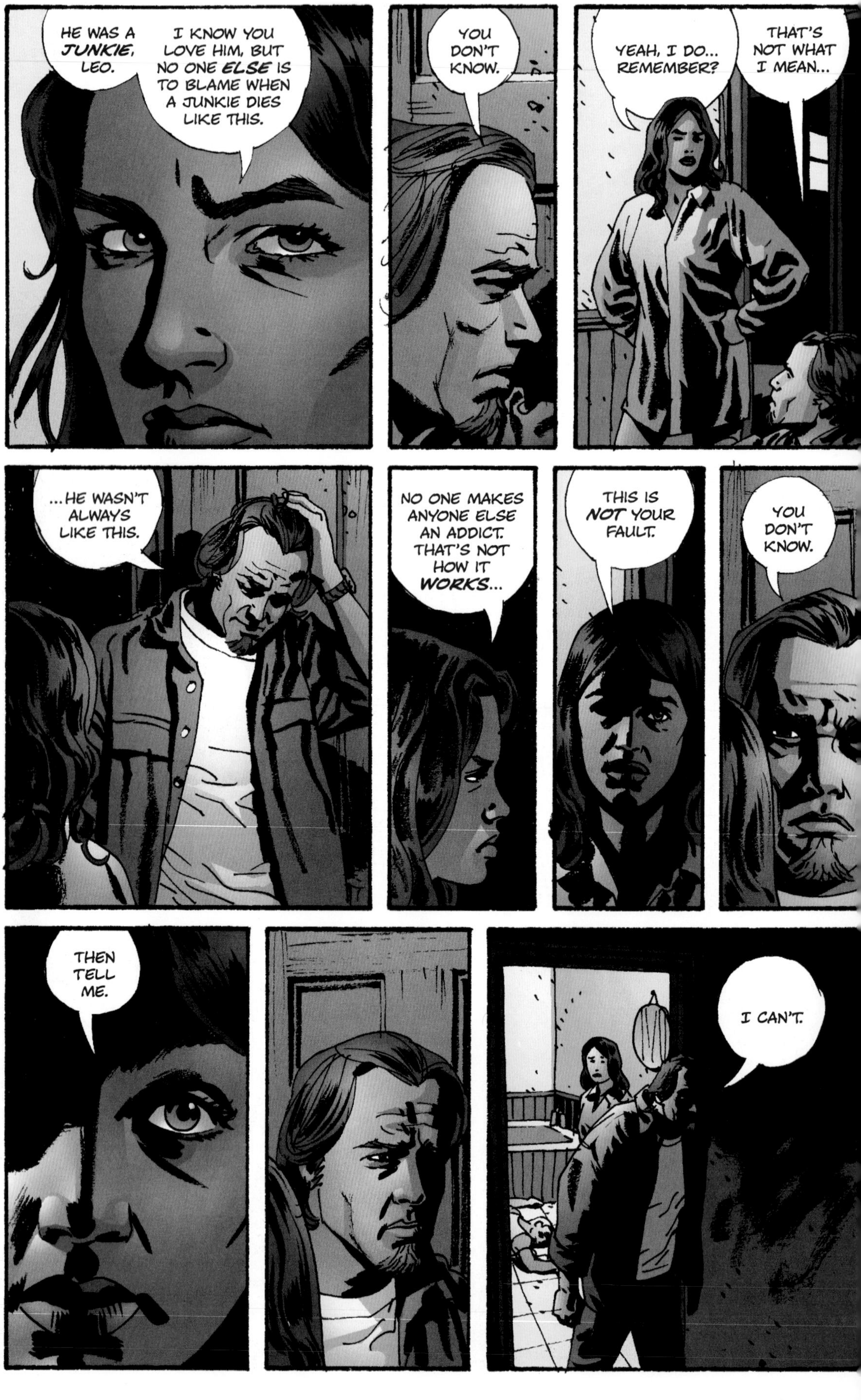

HE WAS A *JUNKIE*, LEO.
I KNOW YOU LOVE HIM, BUT NO ONE *ELSE* IS TO BLAME WHEN A JUNKIE DIES LIKE THIS.
YOU DON'T KNOW.
YEAH, I DO... REMEMBER?
THAT'S NOT WHAT I MEAN...
...HE WASN'T ALWAYS LIKE THIS.
NO ONE MAKES ANYONE ELSE AN ADDICT. THAT'S NOT HOW IT *WORKS*...
THIS IS *NOT* YOUR FAULT.
YOU DON'T KNOW.
THEN TELL ME.
I CAN'T.

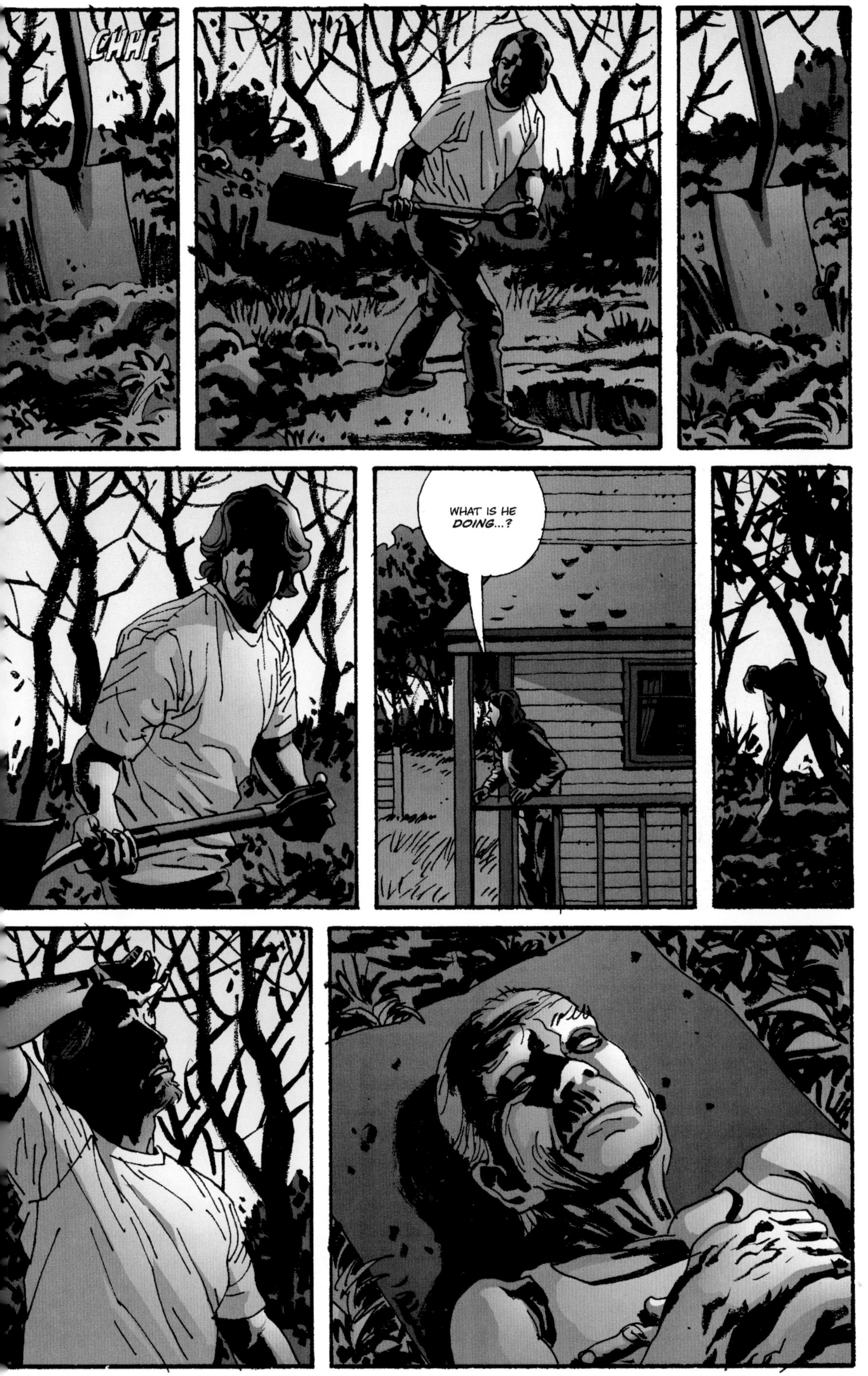
CHHF
WHAT IS HE DOING...?

NO... YOU DON'T BUMP UNLESS YOU *HAVE TO*.

THE *BUMP* IS FOR *AMATEURS*.

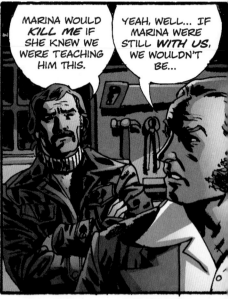

MARINA WOULD *KILL ME* IF SHE KNEW WE WERE TEACHING HIM THIS.

YEAH, WELL... IF MARINA WERE STILL *WITH US*, WE WOULDN'T BE...

BUT THE WAY I SEE IT, TOMMY, YOU'VE GOT TWO CHOICES...

FIND A NEW CAREER...OR TEACH *LEOPOLD* HERE WHAT WE DO.

THE KID'S *LIVING* IN THIS WORLD, MIGHT AS WELL KNOW HOW TO *SURVIVE* IN IT.

HEY UNCLE IVAN... *LOOK!*

OH MY GOD... THE KID'S A *NATURAL.*

BUT YOU *FELT IT*, DIDN'T YOU?

JUST A LITTLE, LEO, JUST A BIT... BUT YOU'VE GOT THE TOUCH.

STOP, KID... JUST STOP.

LISTEN TO ME, IVAN...

...YOU TAKE CARE OF LEO – KEEP HIM *SAFE.*

THAT'S *ALL* I CARE ABOUT. YOU JUST KEEP *HIM* SAFE.

DAD! NO!

DAD!

YOU'RE JUST GOING TO BURY HIM *OUT HERE?*

SERIOUSLY?

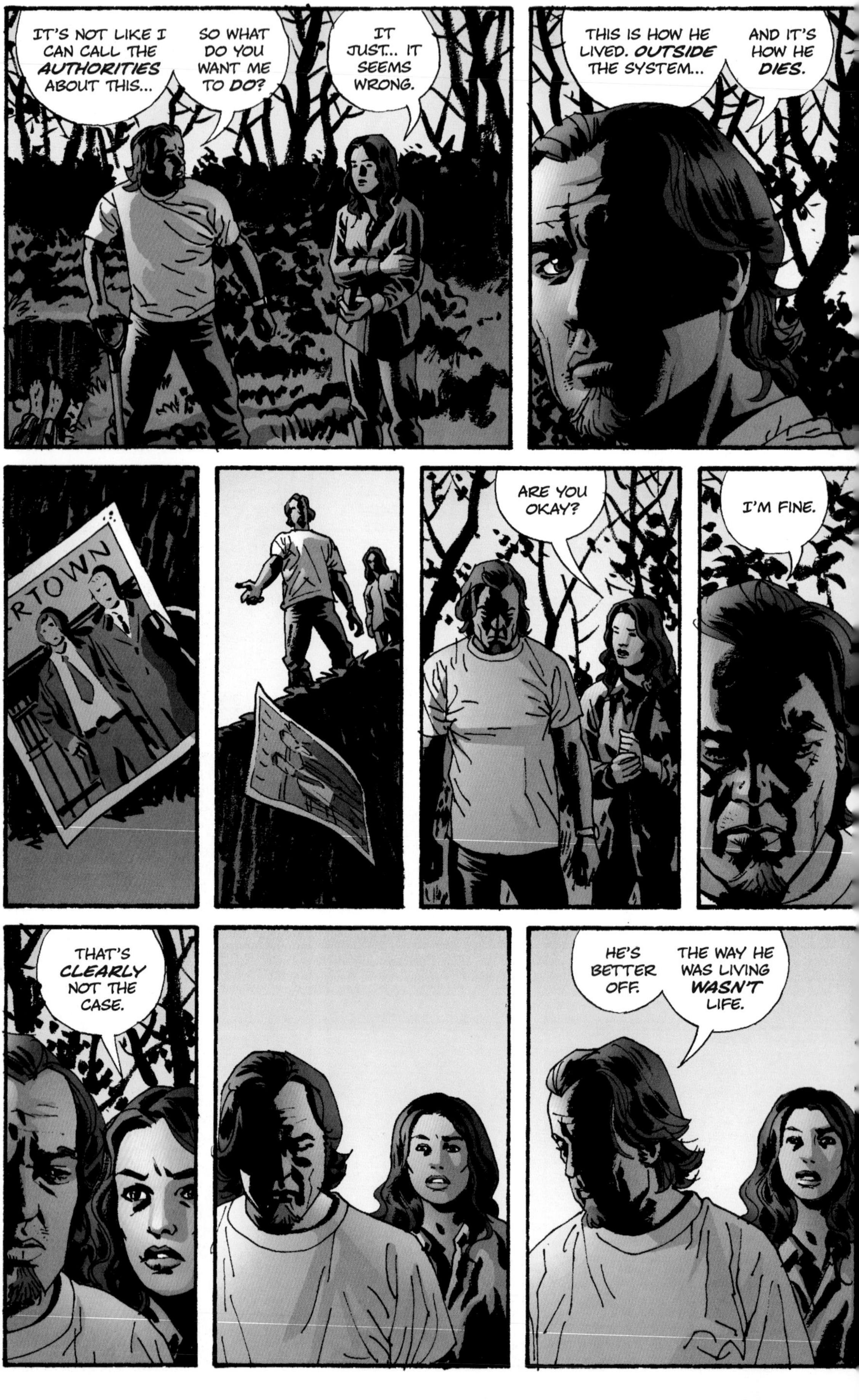

IT'S NOT LIKE I CAN CALL THE *AUTHORITIES* ABOUT THIS...
SO WHAT DO YOU WANT ME TO *DO?*
IT JUST... IT SEEMS WRONG.
THIS IS HOW HE LIVED. *OUTSIDE* THE SYSTEM...
AND IT'S HOW HE *DIES.*
RTOWN
ARE YOU OKAY?
I'M FINE.
THAT'S *CLEARLY* NOT THE CASE.
HE'S BETTER OFF.
THE WAY HE WAS LIVING *WASN'T* LIFE.

YOU DON'T MEAN THAT.

GOD, LEO... YOU *CAN'T* MEAN THAT.

DON'T TELL ME WHAT I MEAN.

JUST 'CAUSE WE *SLEPT TOGETHER*, DON'T THINK YOU KNOW ME.

BUT I'M TRYING TO...

IF YOU'D *FUCKING* LET ME.

I'M TRYING TO *HELP*–

I DON'T *NEED* HELP FROM YOU... OR FROM ANYONE.

GOD *DAMN* YOU. I THOUGHT YOU WERE DIFFERENT.

I THOUGHT THEY WERE *WRONG*.

BUT NOW I GET IT. YOU AREN'T AFRAID OF VIOLENCE OR GUNS OR ANYTHING LIKE THAT...

BUT YOU'RE AFRAID TO *LET ME IN*.

YOU FUCKING *COWARD*.

YOU'RE *LEAVING?* YOU'RE JUST LEAVING?

THIS HAS GONE ON LONG ENOUGH.

I'M GONNA FIND A WAY TO FIX IT.

IF I *CAN*, I'LL GET US FREE OF THIS WITH SOME *CASH* IN OUR POCKETS... AND WE CAN GO OUR SEPARATE WAYS.

YOU CAN GET YOUR DAUGHTER AND GET OUT OF TOWN, LIKE YOU WANTED.

LEO...

JUST SIT TIGHT FOR ONE MORE DAY.

CAN YOU *DO* THAT? PLEASE?

DAMN IT...

DAMN IT DAMN IT DAMN IT...

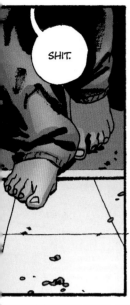
SHIT.

DAMN IT, LEO... WHAT THE HELL DID YOU DO?

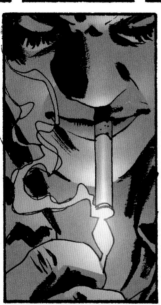

FUCK!

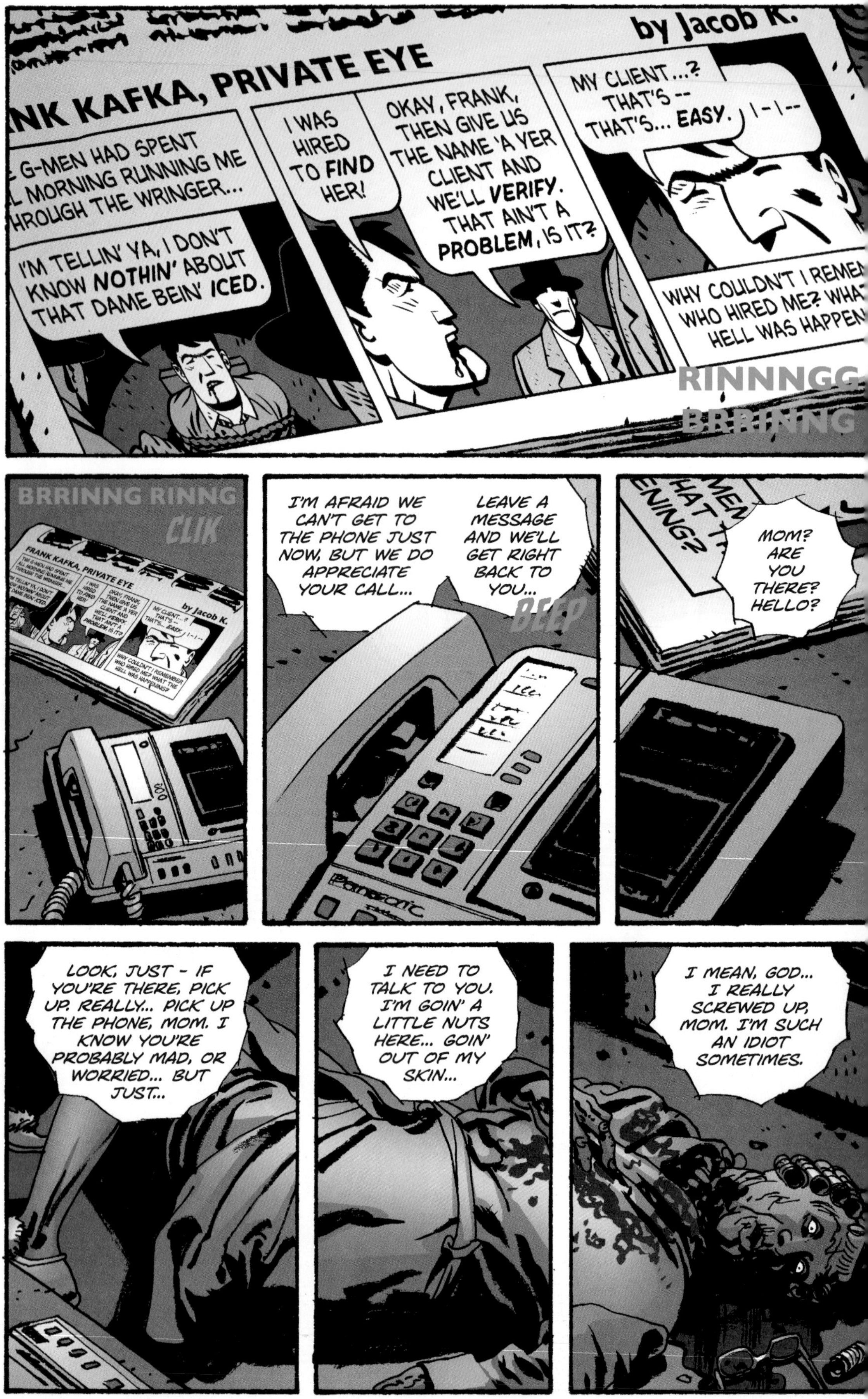
by Jacob K.
NK KAFKA, PRIVATE EYE
E G-MEN HAD SPENT L MORNING RUNNING ME THROUGH THE WRINGER...
I'M TELLIN' YA, I DON'T KNOW NOTHIN' ABOUT THAT DAME BEIN' ICED.
I WAS HIRED TO FIND HER!
OKAY, FRANK, THEN GIVE US THE NAME 'A YER CLIENT AND WE'LL VERIFY. THAT AIN'T A PROBLEM, IS IT?
MY CLIENT...? THAT'S -- THAT'S... EASY. I-I--
WHY COULDN'T I REMEM WHO HIRED ME? WHA HELL WAS HAPPEN
RINNNGG
BRRINNG
BRRINNG RINNG
CLIK
I'M AFRAID WE CAN'T GET TO THE PHONE JUST NOW, BUT WE DO APPRECIATE YOUR CALL...
LEAVE A MESSAGE AND WE'LL GET RIGHT BACK TO YOU...
BEEP
MOM? ARE YOU THERE? HELLO?
LOOK, JUST - IF YOU'RE THERE, PICK UP. REALLY... PICK UP THE PHONE, MOM. I KNOW YOU'RE PROBABLY MAD, OR WORRIED... BUT JUST...
I NEED TO TALK TO YOU. I'M GOIN' A LITTLE NUTS HERE... GOIN' OUT OF MY SKIN...
I MEAN, GOD... I REALLY SCREWED UP, MOM. I'M SUCH AN IDIOT SOMETIMES.

AND NOW... I'M THINKING ABOUT MAKING A WORSE MISTAKE.

AND I **REALLY** DON'T WANNA DO THAT. SO I JUST...

DAMN IT... I'M NOT EVEN **SUPPOSED** TO BE CALLING YOU.

I JUST WANTED TO... WANTED TO HEAR ANGIE'S **VOICE**...

YOU GOT IT?

I'LL JUST... I'LL TRY BACK LATER.

JUST GIMME A SECOND TO RUN IT THROUGH...

GOT IT.

WHERE THE HELL ARE THEY?

SOME LITTLE FARMING VALLEY ABOUT AN HOUR OR TWO OUTSIDE TOWN.

ALL RIGHT. LET'S TAKE THE PICTURE AND THEN YOU CAN CALL YOUR LITTLE BITCH, SEYMOUR.

SMILE, BABY GIRL... THIS IS FOR YOUR MOMMY.

HUH HUH HUH HUH...

THE WHOLE DRIVE BACK TO THE CITY, ALL I CAN THINK IS WHAT AN ASS I WAS, LEAVING IT LIKE THAT.

AND WHEN I GET TIRED OF THINKING ABOUT GRETA, I BEAT MYSELF UP ABOUT IVAN SOME MORE.

IT'S A REGULAR PITY PARTY, BUT THANKFULLY NO ONE ELSE IS INVITED.

BUT BY THE TIME I GET WHERE I NEED TO BE, MY MIND IS ALL ON BUSINESS, WHERE *IT* NEEDS TO BE.

GENUINE JEN... LONG TIME.

LEOPOLD. THE MAN OF THE HOUR... LATE AS USUAL.

YOU LOOK GOOD.

I LOOK FUCKING *GREAT*, ASSHOLE. BUT *YOU* LOOK LIKE SHIT.

UH, LEO... ARE YOU *CARRYING?*

YEAH.

THAT ISN'T LIKE YOU.

I'M ON THE WAY TO SEE A FRIEND.

I THOUGHT *WE* WERE FRIENDS.

THE *OTHER* KIND OF FRIEND.

OH... THE ONES THAT SHOOT YOU IN THE BACK AND TAKE YOUR SCORE.

THOSE AREN'T FRIENDS, LEO.

JENNY WATERS WAS ONE OF THE ORIGINAL GANG, WAY BACK IN HIGH SCHOOL. WE FELL IN TOGETHER BECAUSE OUR PARENTS ALL WORKED IN THE SAME CREW SOMETIMES.

I GUESS, THINKING ABOUT IT, OUR PARENTS WERE THE ORIGINAL GANG... WE WERE THE NEXT GENERATION.

AND FOR MOST OF US, THAT TURNED OUT TO BE TRUE... BUT NOT JENNY. SHE WENT IN THE *OPPOSITE* DIRECTION, DEFIANT AND PROUD.

JENNY WAS NOT ONLY A POLICE DETECTIVE, SHE WORKED *INTERNAL AFFAIRS.* SHE WAS A PARIAH IN EVERY WORLD SHE LIVED IN...

I DIDN'T SEE YOU AT RICKY'S FUNERAL.

YOU WENT TO THAT?

I WATCHED FROM MY CAR, WITH A ZOOM LENS.

HELL, I WOULD'VE GONE IF I'D KNOWN *THAT* WAS AN OPTION.

I LAY OUT MY PROBLEM FOR JENNY, BECAUSE WHEN YOU'RE DEALING WITH CROOKED COPS, THERE'S NO BETTER PLACE TO GO THAN I.A.D.

LEO, YOU *FUCKING* IDIOT. WHY DIDN'T YOU COME TO ME *BEFORE*?

I DON'T KNOW, MAYBE 'CAUSE I'M NOT AN INFORMANT?

DON'T BE AN ASSHOLE.

I JUST DIDN'T *SEE IT* RIGHT, JEN. THOUGHT THEY WERE GONNA TRY TO MUSCLE US OUT *AFTER*.

THEY HAD A WHOLE OTHER PLAN, THOUGH, *OBVIOUSLY*...

YEAH, JEFF DRISCOLL AND HIS CREW HAVE BEEN IN SOMEONE'S POCKET FOR A WHILE NOW.

WE JUST HAVEN'T BEEN SURE *WHOSE* UNTIL RECENTLY.

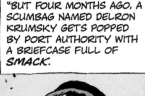

"BUT FOUR MONTHS AGO, A SCUMBAG NAMED DELRON KRUMSKY GETS POPPED BY PORT AUTHORITY WITH A BRIEFCASE FULL OF *SMACK*.

"AND THE NEXT DAY, JEFF'S PARTNER EATS HIS OWN GUN FOR BREAKFAST. DOESN'T EXACTLY TAKE AN OPPENHEIMER TO ADD *THAT* UP."

DELRON WORKS FOR A GUY KNOWN AS *ROY-L*, WHO WAS CLEARLY *NOT* HAPPY TO SEE HIS SPECIAL HEROIN GO BYE BYE.

SPECIAL?

HIGHER PURITY. EASIER TO SMUGGLE, AND YOU CAN STEP ON IT TWICE AS MUCH.

JEFF AND HIS BOYS WERE SUPPOSED TO GET DELRON WAVED THROUGH THE SECURITY CHECK...

...BUT *SOMEONE* FORGOT TO PAY OFF SOMEONE, AND IT ALL FELL TO SHIT.

AND SO JEFF GOES SCRAMBLING TO MAKE SURE HE DOESN'T END UP LIKE HIS PARTNER...

WHICH IS WHERE *SEYMOUR* ENTERS THE PICTURE, AND *YOU* BECOME THE PERFECT FALL GUY.

WHAT? NO... SEYMOUR NEEDED ME FOR THE JOB...

SURE, YOU'RE *GOOD*, LEO, BUT WHAT DID SEYMOUR *KNOW* YOU'D DO?

GET AWAY. YOU *ALWAYS* GET AWAY.

MOTHERFUCK.

BULLETS START FLYING, YOU HEAD FOR THE HILLS, THEY TAKE BACK THEIR SCAG.

MEANWHILE, *CIVILIANS* IN THE TUNNEL SEE ONE OF THE ROBBERS *GETTING AWAY...*

...SO *HE* MUST HAVE GOTTEN AWAY WITH THE *LOOT...* RIGHT?

MOTHERFUCK.

IF YOU HADN'T *ACTUALLY* GOTTEN AWAY WITH THE LOOT, EVERY COP IN THE STATE WOULD BE ON YOUR ASS.

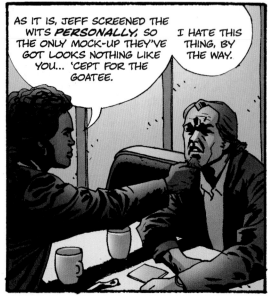

AS IT IS, JEFF SCREENED THE WITS *PERSONALLY*, SO THE ONLY MOCK-UP THEY'VE GOT LOOKS NOTHING LIKE YOU... 'CEPT FOR THE GOATEE.

I HATE THIS THING, BY THE WAY.

SO, ARE YOU PLANNING TO SWOOP ALL THESE BAD PEOPLE UP AND MAKE MY LIFE EASIER?

I WISH.

NO, THE LIEUTENANT WANTS US *WATCHING*, SEEING WHERE ELSE THIS ALL *LEADS*.

HE'S *STILL* HOPING FOR SOME WAY INTO HYDE'S BUSINESS.

DAMN.

SO, WHAT ARE YOU GONNA DO, LEOPOLD?

I HAVE NO IDEA... BUT AT LEAST NOW I KNOW WHERE THE SHIT I'M IN *CAME FROM*. THAT'S SOMETHING...

BE CAREFUL WITH THIS ROY-L AND HIS PEOPLE. THEY'LL KILL YOU JUST FOR *HAVING* THAT SUITCASE.

YOU KNOW DRUG DEALERS AND PIMPS, THEY'RE ALL *PARANOID*.

DON'T WORRY ABOUT ME. I'LL SURVIVE.

I KNOW *THAT*. THAT'S THE *OTHER* THING YOU ALWAYS DO.

BUT HOW EXACTLY WAS I GOING TO GO ABOUT DOING THAT *THIS TIME*? I FIGURED I HAD ONE ANGLE - *SEYMOUR*.

MUCH AS I HATED HANDING A MILLION DOLLAR SCORE TO THE GUY WHO DOUBLE-CROSSED ME... HE WAS THE ONE WHO'D STARTED THIS, AND HE'D HAVE TO END IT.

HE'D HAVE TO TAKE THE SMACK TO HIS PEOPLE AND GET THEM OFF MY BACK.

AND IF HE GOT PAID, THEN MAYBE I'D JUST COME BACK AND ROB HIM.

THAT WAS WHY I BROUGHT THE GUN GRETA HAD GRABBED DURING THE HEIST.

THE MOOD I WAS IN, I WASN'T PLANNING TO TAKE NO FOR AN ANSWER.

BUT HIS APARTMENT IS DARK... AND I DON'T NEED MORE DEAD TIME. MORE TIME TO THINK.

SO I WEIGHT MY OPTIONS... DO I GO TOSS THE PLACE AND THEN WAIT FOR SEYMOUR TO COME HOME?

OR DO I CALL IT A NIGHT AND HEAD BACK TO THE FARM? TRY TO TALK TO GRETA...

...TRY TO EXPLAIN TO HER WHY I'M SO FUCKED UP...

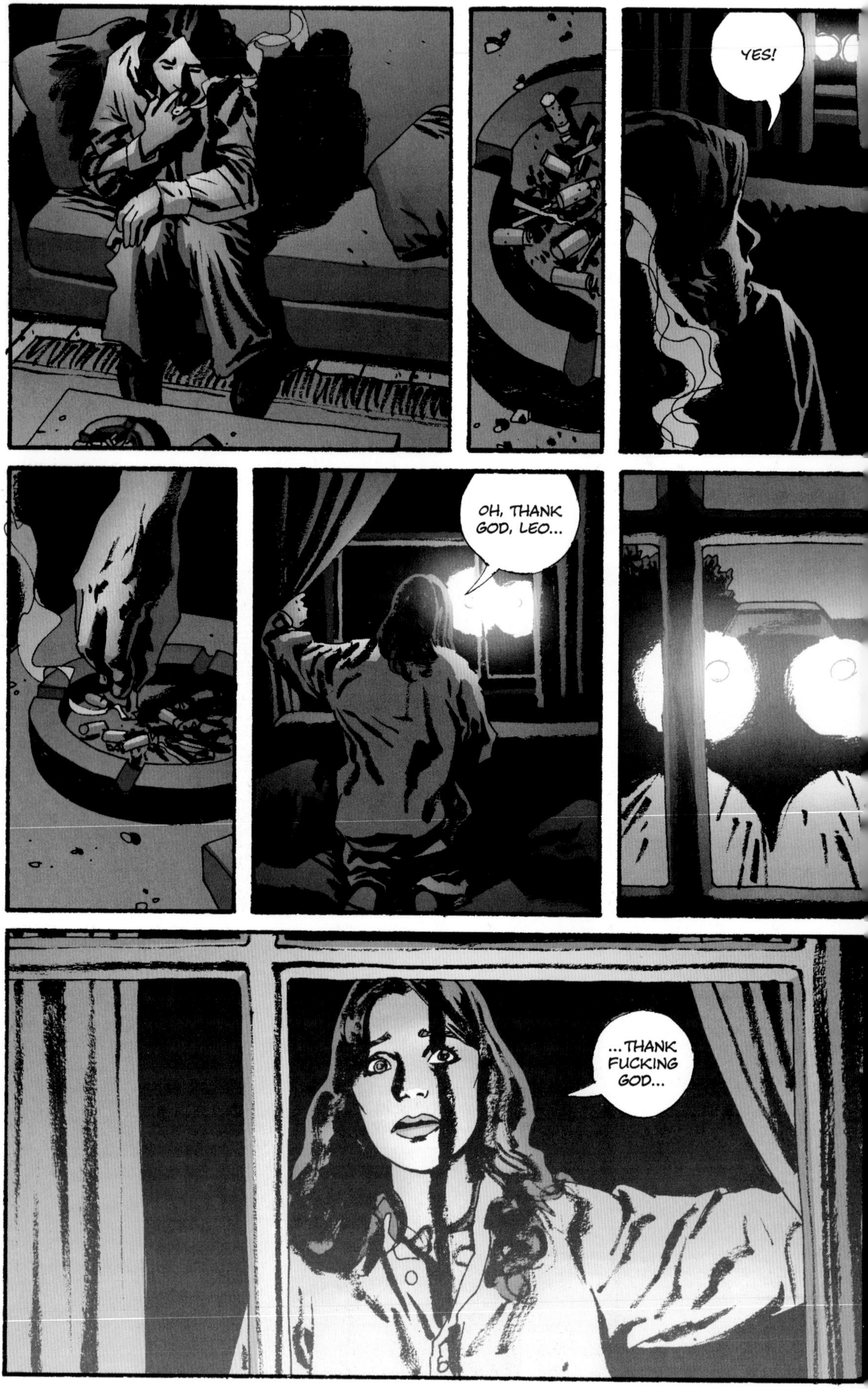
YES!
OH, THANK GOD, LEO...
...THANK FUCKING GOD...

IT TAKES ME ABOUT FIFTEEN MINUTES TO FIND ALL THE MONEY SEYMOUR HAS STASHED AROUND HIS PLACE.

HE KEEPS MOST OF IT ROLLED UP INSIDE CURTAIN RODS, AND IT'S NOT MUCH. A FEW GRAND. I TAKE IT ANYWAY, FOR MY TROUBLE.

BUT I FIND NOTHING ELSE OF INTEREST... NO PHONE NUMBERS, NO HANDWRITTEN NOTES...

NO SIGN THAT JEFF OR THIS ROY-L AND HIS PEOPLE HAVE EVER BEEN HERE...

ALSO NO SIGN OF WHEN SEYMOUR WAS LAST HERE, OR WHEN HE'LL BE COMING BACK.

EXCEPT FOR ONE SMALL FLASHING RED LIGHT.

clik

YOU HAVE ONE MESSAGE... LEFT TODAY, AT 3:47 P.M...

SEYMOUR, IT'S JEFF...

FINALLY GOT A LEAD ON THAT *PACKAGE* WE LOST TRACK OF...

LEO!

...SO NOW YOU AND ME AND OUR NEW *FRIEND* GOTTA TAKE A TRIP OUT TO THE *STICKS*.

NO...

COME ON, MAN, PICK UP...

ALL RIGHT... I'M GONNA TRY YOUR CELL.

OH GOD... NO...

Too Late

NO MATTER HOW FAST YOU DRIVE, TIME JUST STOPS DEAD WHEN YOU KNOW YOU'RE ALREADY TOO LATE.

I'D DRIVEN FROM THE CITY TO MY GRANDFATHER'S FARM HUNDREDS OF TIMES, BUT THIS TIME...

...EVEN WITH THIS OLD HEAP DOING NEARLY A HUNDRED MILES AN HOUR...

...I'M NOTICING THE MOUNTAINS AND THE RIVER I'M NOTICING THE TREES.

I'M NOTICING THE ODOMETER SLOWLY TICKING UP.

I'M TOO LATE.

FOR A MINUTE, WHEN I SEE NO CARS PARKED NEARBY, I THINK MAYBE -- JUST *MAYBE* -- I'M NOT.

BUT IN MY HEART, I KNOW THE TRUTH.

AND IT'S MORE THAN I CAN TAKE.

JESUS...

NO... WHAT DID THEY *DO* TO YOU...?

...I'M SORRY, GRETA... I'M SO --

SORRY ABOUT THE GIRL.

DELRON WASN'T *EASY* TO CONVINCE THE ONLY DOPE *HERE* WAS THAT *ONE BRICK* IN THE UPSTAIRS BATHROOM.

YOU FUCKING BASTARD... YOU DIDN'T HAVE TO DO THIS. ANY OF IT...

HEY. I TRIED TO *SAVE HER*, LEO, I SWEAR.

EVEN THOUGH SHE PRACTICALLY *BROKE MY NOSE* WITH THAT SHOTGUN.

BUT THESE GUYS, THEY JUST... YOU DON'T *KNOW* THESE TYPES OF GUYS.

YEAH, I *DO*, SEYMOUR.

SO, THEY LEFT YOU HERE TO TAKE CARE OF ME?

YEAH. TOLD 'EM YOU WOULDN'T BE ANY TROUBLE.

NOT ONCE I SHOWED YOU *THIS*.

IS THIS --?

GRETA'S DAUGHTER, *ANGIE*. DELRON'S HOLDING ONTO HER, AS AN INSURANCE POLICY.

I GUARANTEED HIM YOU'D GIVE A SHIT, JUST LIKE HER MOM DID...

THE DIFFERENCE BEING **YOU** CAN HAND OVER THE **BRIEFCASE** IN EXCHANGE FOR THE KID.

HELL, HE'S SO FUCKIN' **EXHAUSTED** WITH THIS SHIT, I EVEN CONVINCED HIM TO LET YOU **WALK AWAY.**

WHAT A **FRIEND** YOU ARE...

DON'T.

JUST GET ME THE REST OF THE FUCKING HEROIN.

SO THIS IS YOUR **LIFE** NOW, SEYMOUR? STABBING YOUR OWN KIND IN THE BACK? WORKING WITH PSYCHOS?

THIS IS JUST **ONE** JOB... THAT GOT TOO MESSY FOR ITS OWN GOOD.

YOU DIDN'T HAVE TO LIE TO ME ABOUT THE SCORE.

YOU'D HAVE TAKEN A JOB STEALING A MILLION IN UNCUT **SMACK** FOR A DRUG DEALER?

SEE? I KNOW YOU.

YOU *THINK* YOU DO. A LOT OF PEOPLE DO... BUT YOU DON'T KNOW ANYTHING.

I KNOW YOU'LL DO WHATEVER YOU HAVE TO TO STAY ALIVE... AND IN THE WORLD.

I KNOW THAT EVER SINCE YOUR *DAD* WENT UPSTATE, YOU'VE BEEN TERRIFIED THE SAME THING'LL HAPPEN TO *YOU.*

Y'KNOW, IT'S ALMOST FUNNY. GRETA, *SHE* WANTED TO KNOW... WHAT IT *WAS* I WAS SO AFRAID OF.

AND I COULDN'T *TELL HER,* BECAUSE I JUST... I'VE NEVER TOLD *ANYBODY* WHO WASN'T THERE.

WHAT THE FUCK ARE YOU TALKING ABOUT?

IT'S IN THE TRUNK, CAN I...?

GO AHEAD, JUST... *SLOW.*

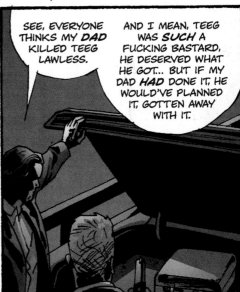

SEE, EVERYONE THINKS MY *DAD* KILLED TEEG LAWLESS.

AND I MEAN, TEEG WAS *SUCH* A FUCKING BASTARD, HE DESERVED WHAT HE GOT... BUT IF MY DAD *HAD* DONE IT, HE WOULD'VE PLANNED IT, GOTTEN AWAY WITH IT.

HE WOULDN'T HAVE STOOD AROUND WAITING FOR THE *COPS.*

OKAY, LET'S SEE IT. AND *NO* BULLSHIT.

SEE?

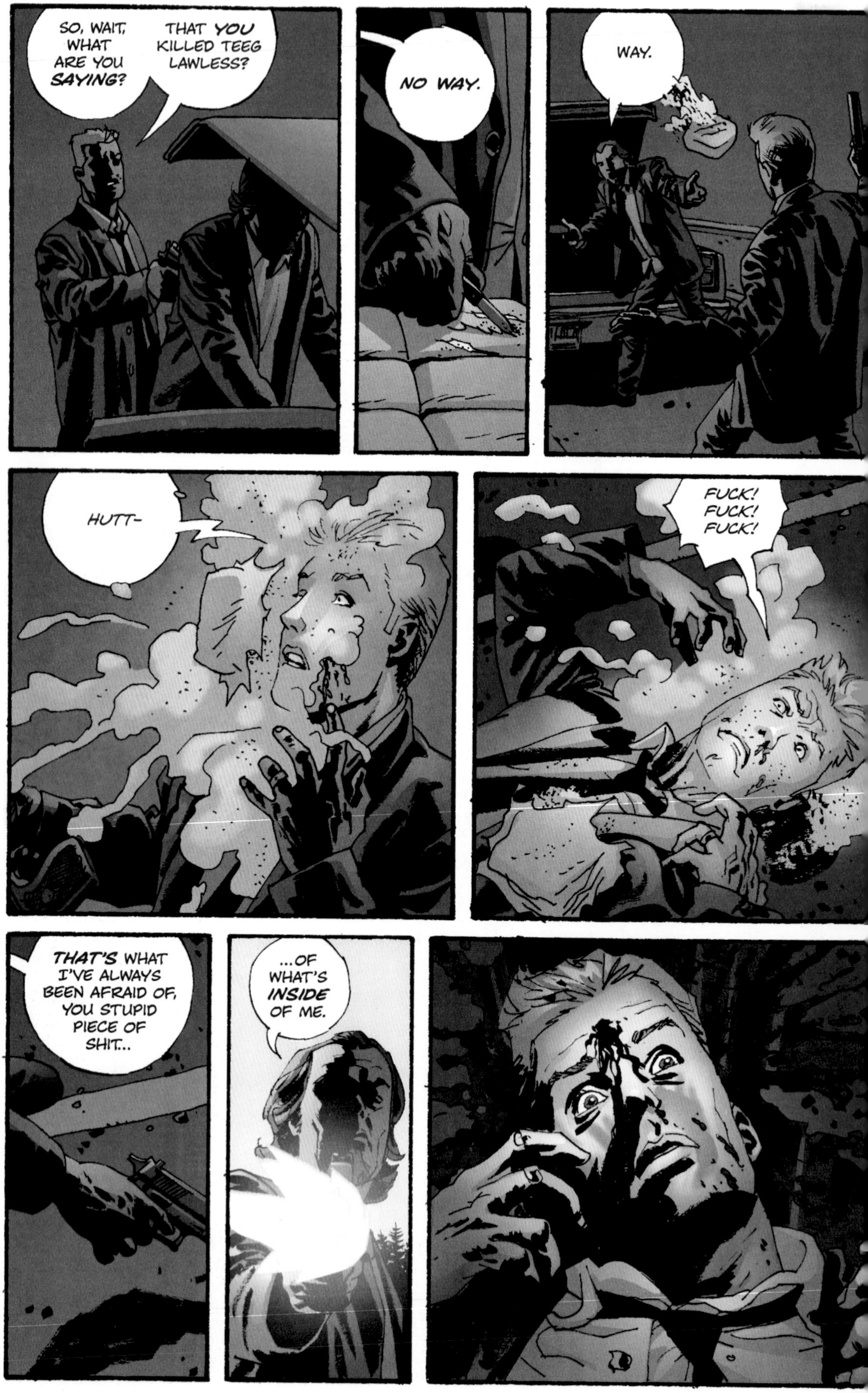
SO, WAIT, WHAT ARE YOU SAYING?
THAT YOU KILLED TEEG LAWLESS?
NO WAY.
WAY.
HUTT-
FUCK! FUCK! FUCK!
THAT'S WHAT I'VE ALWAYS BEEN AFRAID OF, YOU STUPID PIECE OF SHIT...
...OF WHAT'S INSIDE OF ME.

RAGE IS BLIND, AND I'M AN IDIOT. THE MOMENT SEYMOUR'S *A CORPSE*, ALL I CAN THINK ABOUT IS THE GIRL. GRETA'S *KID*.

NO... DAMN IT...

I SHOULD'VE QUESTIONED HIM... BUT WHO KNOWS WHAT A FACE-FULL OF *UNCUT HEROIN* WOULD'VE DONE?

HE MIGHT'VE BEEN GONE ANYWAY, BEFORE I COULD GET A WORD OUT OF HIM.

AS IT IS, I GET LUCKY.

LUCK. *RIGHT.*

EXCEPT, MY LUCK HAS NEVER BEEN ANYTHING BUT A CURSE.

DAMN IT...

THE *VOLUNTEER FIRE DEPARTMENT* AND THE COUNTY'S TWO POLICE CARS PASS ME ON THEIR WAY OUT TO THE FARM.

THE FIRE AND THE BODIES SHOULD KEEP THEM BUSY FOR A WHILE...

...AND GIVE ME TIME TO DO WHAT I HAVE TO IN TOWN.

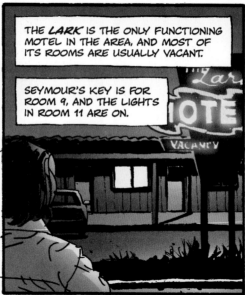

THE *LARK* IS THE ONLY FUNCTIONING MOTEL IN THE AREA, AND MOST OF ITS ROOMS ARE USUALLY VACANT.

SEYMOUR'S KEY IS FOR ROOM 9, AND THE LIGHTS IN ROOM 11 ARE ON.

MY HOPE IS THAT JEFF AND DELRON ARE WAITING HERE, WITH THE GIRL.

I JUST NEED TO MAKE *SURE* BEFORE –

JUST STOP YOUR FUCKIN' MOANIN' YOU LITTLE SHIT!

CHRIST... I CAN'T *WAIT* TO SELL THAT FUCKIN' BRAT...

HEY –

HE'S FASTER THAN HE LOOKS. FUCK.

FUCK.

FUCK.

FUCK YOU THINK YOU WERE GONNA DO, PUSSY?

SHOOT ME?

AAHHH!

YOU JUST MADE THE *BIGGEST MISTAKE* 'A YER SHORT UNHAPPY LIFE!

GONNA GUT YOU LIKE A FUCKIN' BITCH...

WHERE'S MY...?

THE ONE BENEFIT OF A PAINFULLY ACUTE MEMORY IS, ONCE I'M SHOWN SOMETHING, I REMEMBER IT. ALWAYS.

SO I REMEMBER WHERE TO CUT A MAN. WHICH ARTERIES WILL MAKE HIM BLEED OUT QUICK.

HEY... HEY...

THAT WAS ONE OF THE THINGS RICKY LAWLESS' *BROTHER* SHOWED US THE TIME HE CAME HOME ON LEAVE.

IT'S EASIER THAN I THOUGHT IT WOULD BE. BUT IT'S ALWAYS SURPRISED ME HOW MUCH EASIER KILLING IS THAN IT SHOULD BE.

...HEY...

ANOTHER REASON I HATE IT SO MUCH.

AHH... SHIT.

ANGIE?

IT'S OKAY... DON'T SCREAM... I'M NOT HERE TO HURT YOU.

BUH - BUH - WHAT -

EASY, EASY... WHERE'S THE **OTHER** MAN? THE BLACK MAN?

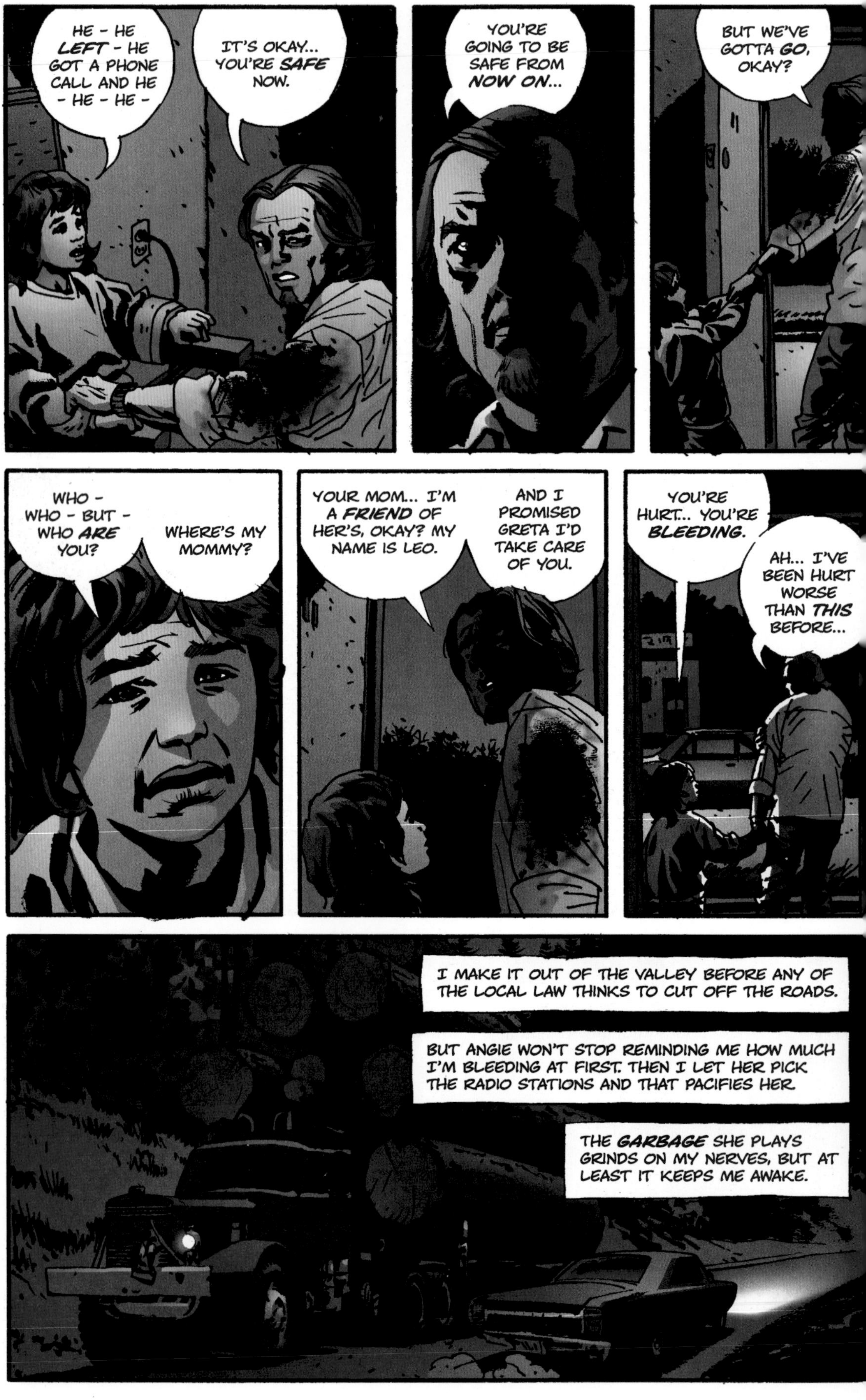
HE - HE LEFT - HE GOT A PHONE CALL AND HE - HE - HE -
IT'S OKAY... YOU'RE SAFE NOW.
YOU'RE GOING TO BE SAFE FROM NOW ON...
BUT WE'VE GOTTA GO, OKAY?
WHO - WHO - BUT - WHO ARE YOU?
WHERE'S MY MOMMY?
YOUR MOM... I'M A FRIEND OF HER'S, OKAY? MY NAME IS LEO.
AND I PROMISED GRETA I'D TAKE CARE OF YOU.
YOU'RE HURT... YOU'RE BLEEDING.
AH... I'VE BEEN HURT WORSE THAN THIS BEFORE...
I MAKE IT OUT OF THE VALLEY BEFORE ANY OF THE LOCAL LAW THINKS TO CUT OFF THE ROADS.
BUT ANGIE WON'T STOP REMINDING ME HOW MUCH I'M BLEEDING AT FIRST. THEN I LET HER PICK THE RADIO STATIONS AND THAT PACIFIES HER.
THE GARBAGE SHE PLAYS GRINDS ON MY NERVES, BUT AT LEAST IT KEEPS ME AWAKE.

I MANAGE TO HANG ON UNTIL I GET TO THE *UNDERTOW*, JUST BARELY...

...AND THANKFULLY I KNOW GNARLY CLEANS UP FOR AN HOUR OR TWO AFTER CLOSING.

HE CALLS IT HIS QUIET TIME.

I ALMOST FEEL BAD BARGING IN ON IT.

KID!

TELL ME YOU STILL HAVE THAT *AWESOME* FIRST AID KIT... PLEASE...

JESUS FUCKING CHRIST, LEO... WHAT'D YOU DO?

...NOT ENOUGH... YET...

UH... KID. WHO'S THE *KID*?

I'M *ANGIE.* WHO ARE *YOU*?

SHE'S *GRETA'S* ... I GOTTA LEAVE HER WITH YOU, GNARLY.

WHAT'RE YOU *TALKIN'* ABOUT? YOU AIN'T GOIN' *ANYWHERE* IN YOUR SHAPE.

IT ISN'T *OVER*... YOU JUST GOTTA HELP ME STOP THIS BLEEDING.

LET ME *REST* A WHILE...

LEO...

CAN YOU HELP HIM, MISTER? HE SAVED ME FROM THE *MONSTERS.*

YEAH, HE'S A REGULAR KNIGHT IN FUCKIN' ARMOR

ALL RIGHT, LET'S GET A LOOK AT THAT CUT...

OAWWW...

AIN'T DEEP, BUT YOU SHOULDN'T'VE *DRIVEN* WITH THIS... STUPID FUCKIN' KID.

LANGUAGE... NOT AROUND THE GIRL. GRETA WOULDN'T LIKE IT.

GUESSIN' I'M NOT GONNA BE *SEEIN'* HER?

NO ONE IS... NO ONE BUT ME...

AND I WAKE FROM A *DREAM* OF HER IN GNARLY'S OFFICE SOMETIME THE NEXT AFTERNOON, FEELING LIKE I'VE BEEN IN A CAR WRECK.

I HEAR GNARLY UPSTAIRS WITH THE KID, PLAYING SOME KIND OF SINGING GAME. I'D LAUGH ABOUT IT, BUT I KNOW IT WOULD HURT TOO MUCH.

SO I RAID THE "LOST AND FOUND" INSTEAD.

EVERYTHING THEY'VE TAKEN OFF MORONS STUPID ENOUGH TO COME IN HERE STRAPPED OR WHO TRY TO SELL DOPE IN THE BATHROOM.

TWO OXYCONTINS AND A FEW LINES OF *CRANK* SHOULD GET ME WHERE I NEED TO BE.

AND SOME OF THE OTHER THINGS IN HERE SHOULD COME IN HANDY, TOO.

I HOPE GNARLY WON'T MIND, BUT I DON'T STICK AROUND TO ASK.

LIKE I TOLD HIM, THIS ISN'T DONE.

SURVIVAL ISN'T ENOUGH ANYMORE.

WHAT THE HELL?

JEFF IS EASY TO FIND. COPS USUALLY ARE. EVEN ONE AS BENT AS *HE* IS HAS TO PUNCH THE CLOCK ONCE IN A WHILE.

PpFFFF...

IT'S ALL HERE. CALL IT EVEN AND LET'S WALK AWAY, NO HARM DONE.

—L

I FIGURE THE TINY SHERIFF'S DEPARTMENT UP NORTH WILL TAKE AT LEAST A *DAY* TO PROCESS DELRON'S PRINTS, SINCE I TOOK ALL HIS I.D.

FUCKIN' PUSSY...

BUT I STILL DON'T HAVE MUCH TIME...

...BEFORE JEFF AND ROY-L REALIZE THEY HAVE *NO IDEA* WHO THEY'RE DEALING WITH.

HE LEADS ME RIGHT TO THE GATES OF HELL AND I WATCH THE GUARD DETAIL AS HE DESCENDS INTO IT.

GET'CHER ASS IN THERE.

DON'T FUCKING TOUCH ME.

LIKE MOST DRUG KINGPINS, ROY-L KEEPS HIMSELF LOCKED UP TIGHT, SAFE -- BUT I SEE A WAY.

THEIR FLAW IS THEY'RE PROTECTING THE PLACE AGAINST A *SQUAD* OF COPS OR RIVALS.

IT WOULD NEVER OCCUR TO THEM THAT *ONE MAN* WOULD TRY TO BREACH THEIR FORTRESS.

HE'D HAVE TO BE CRAZY.

SUICIDAL.

HEY – THAT CAR'S ON *FIRE*. THAT *YOUR* CAR?

AW... *SHIT!*

ROY-L'S VEE!

OUTTA THE FUCKIN' WAY, WHITE BOY!

SHIT!

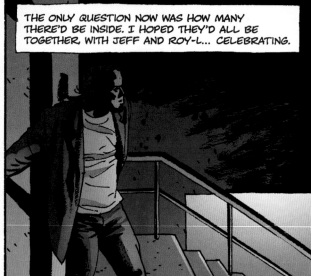

THE ONLY QUESTION NOW WAS HOW MANY THERE'D BE INSIDE. I HOPED THEY'D ALL BE TOGETHER, WITH JEFF AND ROY-L... CELEBRATING.

MOTHERFUCK ME IN THE ASS... YOU CAME THROUGH.

JUST A MATTER OF *TIME*, ROY-L. ALWAYS WAS JUST A MATTER OF TIME.

WHERE OL' DELRON AT?

PROBABLY HANDIN' OFF THAT LITTLE GIRL TO THE *IVANS* OR BEING A COMPLETE PERVERT...

AWRIGHT... LET'S GET THIS SHIT OVER TO MY *GIRLS*... GET SOME *RETURN* ON MY INVESTMENT.

SPEAKING OF THAT... THIS WHOLE OPERATION HAS REALLY SCREWED ME, ROY-L.

INTERNAL AFFAIRS IS ALL IN MY BUSINESS... *ESPECIALLY* SINCE LARRY DISAPPEARED.

HAD TO RUSH BACK TO THE CITY YESTERDAY SO THEY COULD BITCH AT ME FOR A FEW HOURS.

SO, WHAT'S YOUR POINT?

I NEED MONEY. I NEED TO DISAPPEAR MYSELF. THIS ONE JUST GOT *TOO HOT.*

MONEY? YOUR FUCK-UP MADE THIS SHIT GO DOWN.

NOW YOU WANNA GET PAID AGAIN?

FAR AS DISAPPEARIN' GOES... WELL –

PEOPLE KNOW I'M HERE, ROY.

SHIIIT... *WHAT* PEOPLE?

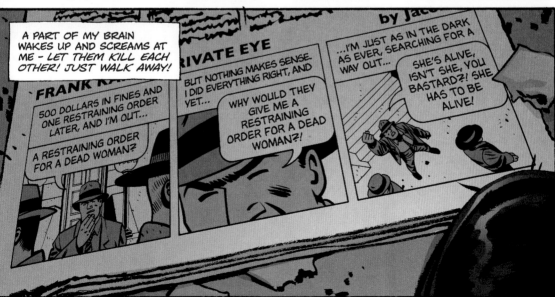

A PART OF MY BRAIN WAKES UP AND SCREAMS AT ME – LET THEM KILL EACH OTHER! JUST WALK AWAY!

by Jac

FRANK KA

RIVATE EYE

500 DOLLARS IN FINES AND ONE RESTRAINING ORDER LATER, AND I'M OUT...

A RESTRAINING ORDER FOR A DEAD WOMAN?

BUT NOTHING MAKES SENSE. I DID EVERYTHING RIGHT, AND YET...

WHY WOULD THEY GIVE ME A RESTRAINING ORDER FOR A DEAD WOMAN?!

...I'M JUST AS IN THE DARK AS EVER, SEARCHING FOR A WAY OUT...

SHE'S ALIVE, ISN'T SHE, YOU BASTARD?! SHE HAS TO BE ALIVE!

BUT I KNEW THE MINUTE I WENT THROUGH THOSE DOORS, THERE WAS NO WALKING BACK OUT.

BECAUSE *I'M* BREAKING THE SAME RULE MY *FATHER* DID...

...AND I COULDN'T STOP MYSELF EVEN IF I WANTED TO.

HEY! MOTHERFU—

--UCK--

GRETA WAS RIGHT. I'M NOT A GOOD SHOT.

THAT'S WHY I GRABBED THE UZI FROM GNARLY'S *LOST AND FOUND.*

WITH THIS, YOU DON'T *HAVE* TO BE GOOD. YOU JUST HAVE TO AIM IN THE RIGHT DIRECTION.

THAT'S THE THEORY, AT LEAST.

SHIT!

AHH!

FUU–

YOU *STUPID* SON OF A BITCH... WHAT WERE YOU THINKIN'?

YOU JUST SAVED MY *LIFE*.

...FU...FUCK ... YOU...

...FU... FU...

LOOKS LIKE YOU HAD MORE *BALLS* THAN BRAINS AFTER ALL... IN THE END.

WHAT THE *FUCK!* ROY -

AIN'T *HERE* NO MORE!

MOTHERFUCKERS...

DISPATCH, THIS IS DETECTIVE CAR 215. OFFICER NEEDS ASSISTANCE.

I'VE GOT A DRUG-RELATED *SHOOTING*, MULTIPLE VICTIMS...

AND I NEED A *BUS*, STAT. I'VE BEEN SHOT.

DETECTIVE 215, CONFIRM *LOCATION*. BACK-UP AND MEDICAL ASSISTANCE ARE *EN ROUTE*.

125th NEAR THE *TRAIN STATION*. TELL THEM TO LOOK FOR THE *FIRE*.

OH, WHAT THE —

...JESUS... WH... WHY...?

...WHY DIDN'T YOU... JUST RUN...?

...BROKE... TOO MANY RULES...

...AND THOSE WERE YOUR... CIGARETTES... YOU BURNED HER...

...AH... I WAS... WAS... WA...

TURNS OUT DYING IS A LOT HARDER THAN KILLING.

A LOT MORE *PAINFUL*, TOO...

...AH... OWW...

THERE'S A SIREN IN THE DISTANCE... LIKE A SONG CALLING ME HOME...

I THINK OF GRETA... HOW SHE'LL NEVER HEAR THAT CALL AGAIN...

BUT THIS SONG IS GETTING LOUDER... STARTING TO SCREAM AT ME...

I CAN'T BE HERE WHEN THE SONG STOPS... I CAN'T BE HERE...

BUT LIKE I SAID, DYING... DYING IS HARDER THAN KILLING...

JUST MY LUCK.

S.W.A.T.

The End

Brubaker Phillips Staples

Acknowledgements

COWARD, and the comic is was serialized in, CRIMINAL, could not have been done without the generous help and support of friends and family, co-workers, and even strangers, and this is where I thank them all: Shane Black for making Kiss Kiss Bang Bang and waking me up again. Sean for drawing it the way I see it in my head. Brian Bendis, Brian Reed, Rich Amtower, John Layman, Matt Fraction, for late-night murder and mayhem. Jim McCann, David Gabriel, Jeff Youngquist, Joe Quesada, Dan Buckley, and everyone else at Marvel that has to deal with our book regularly. Brian and Liz Sendelbach, Jason Lutes and Becca Warren, and their babies, Albin and Clementine, for occasionally getting me out of the house. Ande Parks, Patton Oswalt, David Goyer, Warren Ellis, Greg Rucka, Charlie Huston, and Charles Ardai, for contributing articles and thoughts on noir and crime to the back pages of CRIMINAL. Fraction contributed, too, but I already thanked him before. Robert Kirkman for general advice and for helping us promote the book, and Val Staples for doing everything that we don't, and making the trains run on time, even when they don't let him sleep. And finally, thanks to my wife, Melanie, who doesn't even know how much I could not do any of this without her constant support and care.

Ed Brubaker

I'd like to thank two people who have always been supportive of my work and pushed me to try harder with my comics.
Duncan Fegredo has had to put up with me for years, moaning about comics and the quality of the product out there. Now Ed and I have tried to do something about that, to produce a book we totally believe in, without hopefully adding to that huge mountain of mediocre comics churned out every month. Duncan has offered constructive criticism and inspiration for this book and I'd like to think I can continue bugging him about my comics in the future.
Mostly though I'd like to thank my long-suffering wife Janette for also having to put up with my moaning for years. This book has been all consuming over the past year or so and she's had to take care of everything else while I drew it. Thanks to her for letting me get on with the book, it would all mean nothing without her and Fred, Jake and Archie. Now if only I could get her to actually read it...

Sean Phillips